Crouching Tiger
Taming the Warrior Within

Crouching Tiger

Taming the Warrior Within

by
Loren W. Christensen

  Turtle Press   Hartford

To contact the author or to order additional copies of this book:
Turtle Press
P.O. Box 290206
Wethersfield, CT 06129-0206
1-880-77-TURTL

ISBN 1-880336-69-3
LCCN
Printed in the United States of America

10 9 8 7 6 5 4 3 2 1

To all the warriors who have showed me the way.

Contents

INTRODUCTION

Humans have expressed their warrior spirit through some form of fighting for as long as they have trudged on Earth. When Cain and Abel fought, they probably used dinosaur bones and a few eons later, warring tribes used slings, arrows and catapults. Gunpowder reared its ugly head a few millenniums after that, making fighting a little less personal, which has continued to today, a time when carloads of teenage gangbangers do drive-by shootings with MAC10 machineguns.

We have definitely come a long way in our ability to fight: from exchanging blows with bones to the myriad of sophisticated fighting systems developed in the Orient, to where we are now, with technology so incredible that we can blow entire cities into radioactive dust with the mere poke of a button. In spite of our ability today to construct state-of-the-art high-rise buildings, replace worn hearts with stronger ones, and blend chocolate, caramel and steamed cream for the perfect, yet outrageously-priced yuppie coffee, each of us still carries deep inside a warrior spirit, an inherent quality, not far removed from our prehistoric ancestors.

Our personal warrior spirit may be aggressive, intense, easily unleashed, or it may be quiet and rarely show itself. Within some people, it's buried deeply, the result of profound religious beliefs, psychological factors or other influences. The majority of people, it seems, carry theirs just under the thin veneer of today's societal graces. These people are soldiers, police officers, martial artists, street thugs, athletes, hunters, barroom brawlers, corporate executives, politicians, mothers and fathers. Some are good people and some are not. Some express their warrior spirit with words, laws and money, while others do it with their fists and weapons. Most people have learned to control their warrior spirit, drawing upon it only when absolutely necessary. Others, however, freely express theirs, which is why we have police and prisons, and a military with computer-driven missiles.

As a teenager, I got into three fights that opened my eyes to violence and revealed something inside of me that I didn't know existed. I was unaware of the warrior spirit then, but I was to learn that fighting brought something to the surface that at once intrigued, frightened, fascinated and repelled me.

I was about fifteen years old when I got into my first knock-down-drag-out fistfight in a yellow school bus. I stood toe-to-toe in the aisle with a big, older kid and exchanged a couple dozen face punches with him. Eventually, he knocked me across a seat, straddled me and punched my round, cherubic face at will. Though I was the first to give up, he too was glad to see it end because his eyes, nose and lips were swelling as fast as mine.

Afterwards, everything on my body hurt, but nonetheless I felt a strange exhilaration and a sense of pride for having given my best in a good fight. I lost, but I proved to myself — that voice of self-doubt in the back of my mind — and to those on the bus, that I was not a coward. I wasn't anxious to get into another fight anytime soon, but if one happened, I knew I could give a good account of myself, even if I lost again.

Two years later, my best friend, Mike, and I slugged it out behind a grocery store where we both worked. The hugely one-sided fight lasted twenty minutes, as I punched and kicked him at will. Every time I tried to walk away, he pushed and shoved me to continue. It finally ended with him lying in a fetal position, moaning and spitting up blood.

Later that night, I thought about why I let the fight happen in the first place. Although Mike started it — he was angry with me over something that happened in the store — he was my best friend, so I should have backed away and flatly refused to fight him. But I didn't. I fought him and …I liked it. It was exciting and I liked the strategy and sense of power I felt afterward, feelings that were far more intense than the guilt I had over the fight.

At age nineteen, about five months after I began studying karate, a drunk jumped me in the parking lot of a hamburger joint. The attack was unprovoked and caught me by surprise, but after I got my bearings, I kicked the man in the throat, sending him sprawling over the hood of a car. I leaped on him like a madman, grabbing his hair and repeatedly banging his head against the windshield, which brought screams of terror from the young couple desperately clutching each other in the car. A police officer cruising through the lot, leapt out of his car, pulled us apart and then unwisely stuffed us in his backseat without handcuffing us. Just as he began to interview witnesses, I started punching my attacker in the face, so that the officer had to jump into the back to separate us again. Another police car was summoned and we were taken to jail in separate rides. A month later a judge found him guilty of unprovoked assault.

I learned from this fight that I was capable of great rage, especially when I felt I was being bullied. Once I hurt the man with my kick, I attacked him with ferocity, ignoring his throat injury and his inability to fight back. I was enraged by his attack and I wanted to punish him for it. If it hadn't been for the police officer stopping me, I don't know how far I would have gone.

I had never before felt this extraordinary rage and aggression, and it concerned and frightened me. I didn't know what it was until several months into my martial arts training when I learned about a thing called warrior spirit, a powerful force within all of us that is neither good or bad, though it can be used for both.

I learned that the hellish German SS and the brutal soldiers of the Khmer Rouge probably saw themselves as noble warriors, though they used their warrior spirit to kill millions. The common barroom bully uses his warrior spirit to pick fights and deliberately hurt people to prove to himself and others that he is superior. Prisons are full of such people who have expressed their warrior spirit this way.

Conversely, people who learn to channel their warrior spirit for good are those who recognize its existence and understand that it can be used for something positive. They may not call it warrior spirit, but they know they have to "burn off some energy" or "let off some steam." Some find that sports are a positive outlet, especially games where they can hit something, like racquetball, tennis, football and the martial arts. Other people use nonphysical outlets, such as aggressive sales techniques, assertive news reporting, boardroom politics or the excitement of profit making on the stock exchange. It really doesn't matter whether the outlet is physical or nonphysical as long as it fits the individual's need to express his or her warrior spirit.

I have studied and taught the martial arts since 1965. I was a soldier in Vietnam and I served in law enforcement for twenty-nine years. As a martial artist, I have taught thousands of students, competed in more than one hundred tournaments and have been fortunate to have trained with a few true martial arts masters. As a police officer, I have been involved in shootings, riots and mass civil disobedience. I have worked as a bodyguard for presidents, vice presidents, an assortment of political candidates, notorious criminals and other "VIPs." Indeed, the path I have traveled throughout my life has required me to call upon my warrior spirit over and over. Not always for the good.

This book contains some of the occurrences that have helped me to understand my warrior spirit, at least a little. Sometimes I've made a mistake and thought I had learned a lesson but then turned right around and made the same one again. Most often, I'm happy to report, I've corrected my mistakes and gone on to make new ones.

Within this small volume are anecdotes of times when I was heroic, stupid, fearful, and when my warrior spirit was clearly out of control. I'm proud of some of the experiences that I share in this book and embarrassed by others. I have included the latter because I think it's important to explore all sides of this tremendous force.

While these are my experiences, it's my hope that you will find in some of them, a little or a whole lot of yourself. If they help you to begin understanding your warrior spirit, my efforts have not been wasted.

CHAPTER ONE

Learning at the Expense of Others

Making mistakes is part of life, part of the growing process. We may not like making them and some of us may not admit making them, nonetheless we all do, and the best we can hope for is that no one gets hurt as we stumble through them.

The stories in this section are instances where I lacked control of my warrior spirit, causing me to overreact, exercise poor judgment and abuse my power, which unfortunately resulted in people getting hurt.

When I teach karate to children, I sit them down and talk about what it is that I'm giving them. "When people become police officers," I say, "they are given a gun. The new officers not only learn how to shoot it, but they learn how to be responsible with it, too. They learn how to handle it safely, when to use it and when not to. This responsibility is important because the power of a gun can hurt or kill someone." The children always nod solemnly as they listen, especially when I say, "When I teach you karate, I'm giving you a weapon to defend yourself with. So, I'm going to teach you how to be responsible with your weapon, just like police officers have to learn to be responsible with their weapons." The kids love this comparison and it's apparent by their serious expressions that it has meaning for them.

It's a simple concept, really, so simple that maybe even adults who wield great power, in a myriad of forms, can learn from it, too. Whether a corporate president, a police officer or a person who can kick eighty miles an hour, power is only bad when it's used for that person's personal gain.

I must admit that there were other moments similar to the ones I tell here when I used my warrior spirit abusively. I'm ashamed of all of them, but I think I have learned and grown from the experiences. Happily, there haven't been any lately.

HOWARD

I met Howard in grade school when I was in sixth grade and he was in fifth. He and I and about ten other boys grew up in a part of Vancouver, Washington, called Fruit Valley. We called ourselves the Valley Boys; we weren't a gang, but just a bunch of guys growing up in the 1950s and 1960s. We played war in our backyards, rode our bikes around the suburban streets of Fruit Valley and explored the beach along the Columbia River.

Howard had a mop of dirty blond hair, a stubby, runtish body and he liked to act crazy to get laughs. He also stuttered. He didn't stutter around the Valley Boys, but when his parents were near, especially his father, he stuttered up a storm. He did poorly in school and he had to take second grade twice.

We all picked on Howard, starting in grade school and continuing all the way through middle school, because doing so made us laugh and he was an easy target. While it was just good-natured teasing, it had a tinge of cruelty, too, that trait so many young boys have and that some never grow out of.

We loved to wrestle, and when it was with Howard, we always threw him to the ground a little harder than we did the other Valley Boys. He didn't seem to mind and he always hammed it up as to how hurt he was to get us to laugh. Even when the wrestling got especially rough, Howard always came back for more, accepting everything we did to him without complaint.

16

Years later, after I had read a couple of psychology books, I thought about Howard, remembering how he hated going home, especially when his father was there, and how he loved being with the Valley Boys no matter how we banged him around. We may have tormented him without mercy, but to him we were a family, and he knew we loved him in the way that young boys care about each other.

By 1966 the conflict in Vietnam was escalating, though none of us knew it because we were too busy being teenagers to read the newspapers. Some of the guys were busy finishing their senior year in high school, while a couple of others had finished and were getting jobs. I was the only one going to college. I was also working part-time in a grocery store and spending the rest of my time practicing karate. Howard was still in school but hated it. He quit in his junior year. No longer in the loop with his school friends, unemployable and miserable at home, he joined the Marine Corps.

Howard had been gone for a year when one day I got a call from Richard, one of the Valley Boys. He said Howard was home on leave from the marines and a few of the guys from the old gang were getting together to knock back some beers.

That night at Richard's house, we were all shocked to see how he had changed. He looked older and he had grown taller and heavier. There was an air of maturity about him, too, a new confidence. Even his voice was deeper.

Since a couple of the other guys were thinking about signing up for the marines, Howard was intriguing with his tales of boot camp and the advanced training school. He told us he had received eight hours of intensified hand-to-hand combat training and believed that he could easily destroy anyone who messed with him. He was glad for all the training, he said, because he had just gotten orders to go to Vietnam.

In the year and a half that I had been studying karate, I had advanced through several colored belts and was training hard for the coveted brown belt, the last color before black. I was twenty years old, good at karate, and not just a tad cocky. I told Howard that eight hours of training was insignificant and that I trained more than that in a week. I told him that he was brainwashed and I mentioned a magazine article that said marine boot camp was all about convincing young, impressionable men that they were the toughest fighting force on Earth. I argued that he might be in shape from all the running and push-ups, but he wasn't any match for a karate man.

Howard's face flushed with anger. He jabbed his finger at me and proclaimed loudly that his techniques were for killing and designed to take out the enemy, not for playing tag like karate sparring. That made me angry. I jumped up and told Howard to show me one of his — I spat out the words — "killing techniques." The other guys, who were three or four beers into the evening, shouted encouragement for him to do it.

Howard leaped to his feet and assumed a corny stance used by movie actors who pretend to know karate. "What is that?" I mocked. Enraged, he lunged. I grabbed his arm, swept his feet out from under him and dumped him onto the floor.

Everyone roared with laughter at how comically he had fallen. Suddenly, we were all ten years old again, and ol' Howard had just been thrown once more onto the school playground. This time, though, Howard wasn't laughing and he hadn't been trying to look funny when he fell.

He scrambled to his feet, his face flushed and tight as he angrily brushed off the seat of his pants. He wasn't physically hurt, but there was obvious pain in his eyes as he looked at each one of us.

I, on the other hand, felt good. I had proven I was right about the absurdity of eight hours of hand-to-hand training, the superiority of karate and especially my superiority. His embarrassment was irrelevant because we were all ten years old and it was only Howard. A few minutes later he had his coat on and was walking toward the door. No one acknowledged the tension in the room as we shook his hand and wished him good luck.

After he left, we downed more beers and talked about brainwashed marines, the ineffectiveness of eight hours of hand-to-hand combat and the superiority of karate.

One night, about a month later, my mother greeted me at the door as I returned home from work and told me that I had better sit down. She said she had just received a telephone call from a neighbor...Howard had been killed in Vietnam. He had been in the country less than two weeks, based on some unnamed hill, when a rocket attack slammed into his camp, dead center.

My mother told me later that my head had literally snapped back when she had given me the news. I do remember collapsing into a chair as her words burned into my brain: Howard had been killed...Howard had been killed...Howard...killed. An ice-cold wind swirled up my spine. My eyes teared and I couldn't breathe.

Then I remembered that evening a few weeks earlier when I had last seen him. How I had embarrassed him.

For the next several weeks, I thought a lot about Howard and how I had treated him that night. I asked myself a lot of questions and I didn't like the answers. Why did I feel a need to pop his bubble like that, to treat him with such disrespect? Why didn't I just let him feel good about himself? He had moved beyond the Valley Boys and his parents, as he discovered self-worth as a Marine in the Corps. He had grown, matured and was no longer the runt of the group. Why hadn't I let him bask in his accomplishment and feel good about himself? I hadn't been defending myself that night; I had just flaunted my power.

I thought about what my instructor had said when I first began training. "Along with expertise in the martial arts comes confidence. If you truly are skilled and confident, you don't need to show your abilities unnecessarily. Only a person who lacks confidence has a need to try to impress others by showing off and bullying."

The issue that night wasn't his marine training versus my karate training. What was at issue was my feeling threatened by Howard. He had gone away and, as a result of his experiences and training, had grown and matured far more than I. He had moved beyond the Valley Boys and I was still there, feeling stagnate. Because of my immaturity and lack of confidence, I needed to show him that I was still his superior. And I needed to convince myself, too.

The more I thought about it in the days after his death, the more I realized that I was not an expert in the martial arts as I had thought. I still had a long ways to go and a lot to learn. Sadly, I had embarrassed a friend in the process.

A friend who would never hear my apology.

THE PUNCH

My partner and I had been on patrol for a couple of hours when dispatch told us to meet a sergeant half a block away from Kim's Steam Bath House, an off-limits joint for American servicemen, and one of the many brothels that lined Tu Do Street, a noisy, heavily traveled strip on the edge of Saigon.

I had been working as a military policeman in Vietnam for about six months, so I knew such an order meant there was going to be a raid, a moment of madness when MPs charged a brothel as prostitutes and American servicemen fled out doors and windows. The Vietnamese police would grab the ladies and the MPs would grab the American servicemen, which the MPs always grumbled about as unfair.

We met the sergeant and five other two-man MP jeeps in an alley off Tu Do Street. The sergeant said he had been watching Kim's for the last hour and estimated that there were about forty Americans inside. He wanted us to flip on our sirens as we approached so that most of them would flee, which would happily reduce our paperwork. He was a good sergeant, a man who understood that we couldn't do anything about prostitution and its attraction to servicemen, but we could do something about paperwork.

A few minutes later we arrived in front of Kim's, sirens wailing, tires screeching and voices bellowing, "Military Police!" Several of us remained outside while the others burst through the front doors, shouting orders at prostitutes, who were angry because they hadn't yet been paid and at startled servicemen, who realized they had been caught in an area that was off limits. Some of the servicemen fought, upholding the tradition of what servicemen and MPs have done for years, while others chose not to resist, no doubt feeling vulnerable in their nakedness.

We tried to grab them as they fled out the doors and dived through windows, but it was like trying to catch piglets spilled from a cardboard box. Some of the "piglets," however, weighed over 200 pounds and wore Green Berets. Still, we managed to catch a few.

Most MPs felt that the servicemen we nabbed or scared off in the raids weren't criminals committing heinous crimes, but men seeking a few moments of pleasure in a horrific land. True, they were in an off-limits area, but then the whole country should have been declared off limits. Servicemen who had the proper paperwork to be in Saigon but got sidetracked by the lure of a pretty girl, were usually just given a warning by the MPs and let go. The majority of them appreciated the leniency, but there were always a few who were mean drunk, or just plain mean. That's when the fighting started. As an MP in Saigon, it was virtually impossible to get through a twelve-hour shift without getting into at least one brawl, a fact we just shrugged off as part of the job. On a brothel raid, we expected several.

As a martial artist, I became quickly aware that my three years of karate training in the United States had not prepared me mentally for the brutality and ugliness of real fighting. Some martial arts schools do a good job of training the mind along with the body, but my school didn't. I wasn't taught responsibility with my physical skill, nor was I taught a code of ethics or a warrior philosophy. I was simply trained to fight. Finding myself halfway around the world in a violent, hellish place, I often fought with out-of-control abandon. Since I wasn't mentally prepared for the experience, my fear, lack of confidence and anger often made me careless with my "weapon," my fighting art.

It didn't take me long to develop a street mentality, a philosophy of "kick ass and get their names later." Sometimes I didn't even bother getting names. When I caught a serviceman who had broken the law, I often perceived it as a personal affront and dealt with him as if I was defending my honor rather than doing my job as a police officer. I approached every situation more than ready to unleash my fury should I get even the slightest resistance.

I don't know where this attitude came from. Maybe it was a result of being suddenly thrust into a war zone and having to deal with violence day after day. Maybe it was because I was always scared and my confidence level was constantly fluctuating from extreme highs to extreme lows. Perhaps it was because I was like most young servicemen in Vietnam, who suddenly found themselves stripped of mom, home and apple pie, only to find a violent stranger underneath with an uncontrolled warrior spirit. Whatever the reason, I didn't have time to think about it then since I was smack in the middle of it and far too busy trying to get through each day without getting hurt. In doing so, sometimes I hurt people needlessly.

The first man I grabbed as he ran out the door started to resist but changed his mind when he saw all the jeeps with flashing red lights and all the MPs just waiting for him to put up a fuss. I led the man by his arm over to two MPs assigned to guard prisoners and then returned to the door of the brothel just as a skinny MP stumbled out backwards, struggling with a thickly built marine.

I grabbed the marine's arm, jerked him away from the skinny MP and pushed him hard against a chain link fence. Just as I reached for his arm, another marine, perhaps his buddy, sprinted from out of the shadows toward me, flapping his arms and screaming like a banshee. I struggled to hold my squirming man against the fence and set myself to kick the other one when he got close enough. The skinny MP and the sergeant, however, were on the ball and intercepted the banshee, riding him to the ground like a couple of cowboys with a spirited steer.

I turned my attention back on my guy, who had switched from resisting to cursing the army, my family and me. Police officers should never take such diatribe personally, but I was young, fairly new at the job and undisciplined. I removed my hand from his chest and stepped back, an unwise move since I was giving up what little control I had. He cranked up the volume of his shouts and included some flying spittle and threats to rip me apart, which made my adrenaline bubble; it reached full boil just as he stepped toward me.

I pushed hard against his chest with both hands. It must have caught him off balance, because for a big man he flew backwards easily, landing flat against the chain link fence, sinking into it like a pro wrestler does when he is thrown into the ropes. Then the fence launched him right back toward me. The entire action happened quickly, but I reacted with an explosive corkscrew punch into his chest, right over his heart. This was my strongest hand technique and I drove it in hard, backed by all of my 200 pounds.

The marine's arms shot upward, as if he were the victim of a street hold-up, and he swayed drunkenly on his feet, his mouth opening and closing like a beached fish. His eyes widened and then bulged as if at any moment they would burst from his skull, and then he crumpled straight to the ground, his hands digging at the front of his shirt, as he twitched and shook into a fetal curl.

I ran to the nearest jeep, grabbed the radio mike and screamed in near panic for dispatch to send a medic. I threw the mike on the seat and ran back to the fallen marine, pushing through several MPs who had encircled him. The man had curled into a tight ball, his eyes partially closed and his breathing ragged and rattling.

"What if I've killed him?" I whispered. "What if I've killed him?"

When the ambulance arrived, the medics worked fast to keep the marine breathing. I told them what had happened, feeling a heavy sense of dread and guilt. If only I could back time up ten minutes, I thought.

The medics worked quickly, their faces somber; a couple of times they shook their heads. "What? Why are you shaking your heads?" I asked, but they ignored me and kept working. A moment later one of them said that the man's heart was fibrillating (erratic, rapid heart beats), and that his breathing was getting more shallow. They loaded him onto a stretcher, set him in the ambulance and sped off, siren screaming.

Rumors flew during the next few hours. First, I was told that the marine had gone into cardiac arrest and died, but a few minutes later someone said he was alive and in intensive care. I was assured by all my bearer-of-bad-news buddies that I would be arrested if the marine died, which was true, though I didn't want to hear that right then.

A few hours later, the official word came down that the man was in the hospital and would be flown back to the United States for special care. "Thank God," I whispered.

Whether I was justified in punching the marine is debatable. Punching someone as a police control technique was acceptable in those days, though today it would be considered excessive force unless the officer was fighting for his survival. But I was thinking of neither when I drove my fist into him. What was in my mind was that my assigned authority didn't intimidate him. By hitting him, I wanted him to see me as his superior and I wanted him to be fearful of the MPs.

When I thought about it in the days that followed, hurting him didn't make me feel strong at all — it made me feel small and ashamed.

I also thought about how a bad decision made in haste and for all the wrong reasons can quickly and dramatically affect lives. If the medics hadn't been there, the marine's young life might have ended. I would have been labeled a "killer" and whisked off to prison, changing the direction of my life forever.

OUT OF CONTROL

Dispatch said to see the sergeant at the Saigon jail about picking up a guy to transport to the prison in Long Binh. Since Long Binh was about 35 miles from Saigon, Brett and I were pleased to get the call because it would eat up the entire day. We always enjoyed the drive to Long Binh and back because the country air was fresh and we found the rice paddies and rich green of the countryside to be a nice break from the sweltering concrete and stench of Saigon.

We needed the break, too. Ten months of military police duty in the busiest, most polluted, crowded and violent city in the world had pushed us to the breaking point. We didn't know a thing about stress in those days, but looking back on it now I can see that I was near the end of a rapidly burning fuse. Even the occasional good night's sleep didn't help my aching physical fatigue; my brain as well as my spirit were toasted from working twelve- to sixteen-hour shifts. In ten months, we had enjoyed a grand total of two days off.

The Vietnamese as well as most American servicemen hated our guts. The bold, white "MP" letters on our black helmets and black armbands, and the authority that these gave us, made us the constant targets of verbal insults, physical assaults and even an occasional sniper round. The job was violent, dangerous and frightening. Making all this even worse was that sleep, even on a good night, was fitful because of the oppressive heat, noise and constant buzz of activity.

Although happy to get the radio call to transport the prisoner, I was in a cranky and miserable mood. I had jungle rot on my toes, ringworm on my butt, an old sprained finger that wouldn't heal, and I was nauseous and wilted from the day's one hundred-degree-plus temperature. During the past two days I had been in four fights, been puked on by a drunken sailor, spit on by a doped up marine, chewed out by my sergeant for knocking the spitter on his rear, and a Vietnamese policeman had pulled his gun on me because I had tried to get an American soldier's money back from a prostitute who had rolled him.

I was in a black mood and Brett wasn't feeling any better.

The desk sergeant was waiting for us in the compound area, one of his beefy hands gripping the arm of a skinny, pimply-faced kid. We climbed out of the jeep and walked up to the sergeant, who greeted us with a nod; the kid sneered his lip and looked at Brett and I as though we were mess hall garbage cans. His shirt was without shoulder patches and his brown hair was as long as a hippy's, which indicated he had been hiding in the back alleys of Saigon for a few months. The sergeant said that he had refused his name and from which unit he was AWOL. I instantly disliked the kid, especially the way he was looking me up and down with contempt.

We replaced the sergeant's handcuffs with ours and helped the prisoner into the backseat of our jeep, all the while he continued smirking. I told him to knock it off, but he didn't, adding a few snorts to underscore his disdain. Brett slid in behind the wheel and I sat in the front passenger seat, turned partially so I could keep an eye on the prisoner. We threw the sergeant a mock salute and headed out of the compound.

Thirty minutes later, we had progressed no farther than a mile from the jail. Saigon's exhaust-choked traffic was especially bad and for the umpteenth time that day, we were caught in an immovable jam of bicycles, motorcycles, military vehicles, taxis and a cacophony of horns, engines and curses. Everyone had a ride but no one was going anywhere.

A monster-sized, Vietnamese army truck inched alongside of us. Every few seconds the impatient driver leaned his forearm on the horn, sending out a twenty-second, eardrum shattering blast, which didn't help the jam but did make Brett and I angry. We yelled at the driver to knock it off or we would rip his horn out and stick it where it would make him walk funny. The driver yelled something back in Vietnamese and, though we didn't understand, it was clear that it wasn't nice. As I started to say something back, our jeep rock slightly.

My gut instinct told me instantly what had caused the movement even before I even twisted around and looked dumbly at the empty backseat. "He's escaped!" I yelled.

"There," Brett said, pointing at the jam of traffic behind us. "He's running around that bus."

That was all it took to bring my rage, stress and fatigue together like a thunderclap. I leapt from the jeep with a loud curse. Losing a prisoner was at the top of the list of embarrassing things that could happen to a military policeman.

I zigzagged through traffic, trying not to lose sight of the kid. I executed a perfect two-handed vault over the hood of a taxi but rammed into a motorcycle, knocking it, the old man straddling it, and all his baskets to the pavement. I muttered "Sorry" and sprinted off.

When the kid ran into a less congested alley, the distance between us began to increase. His hands had been cuffed behind his back, but somehow he had maneuvered them to his front. He was at least a half block away now and just as I thought he might elude us, one of his laceless boots flew off, making him stumble. He regained his balance quickly and sped up in spite of his hobble.

I drew my .45 semiautomatic, thinking that the whine of a bullet over his head would scare him into giving up. I aimed as best I could while running and squeezed the trigger. The Colt jammed.

Bam! A shot came from behind me.

I instinctively ducked and twisted around, worrying for a moment that the prisoner had an ally. It was Brett, running right on my heels, holding his .45 in the air; he squeezed off a couple more rounds. *Bam! Bam!*

When I turned back, the kid had stumbled and fallen, a swirl of dust lifting into the air around him. Dozens of Vietnamese, who had been walking, riding their bicycles or just socializing in the alley, fled in every direction, no doubt convinced they were in the middle of a firefight, not with the Viet Cong, but one between crazy American servicemen.

I reached the prisoner just as he was trying to climb to his feet. A hard kick sent him head over heels into the dirt, and follow-up kicks kept him from getting up. When Brett caught up a few seconds later, we both rained wild punches and kicks on him. The kid fought back desperately with his cuffed hands and bare feet, not in an attempt to escape, but to survive our terrible onslaught. The more he fought to defend himself, the more we attacked, as if possessed. We yelled and cursed and punched and kicked. As his fight began to weaken, ours grew stronger, but only for a moment before Brett and I grew so weak we could beat him no more. Spent, we collapsed across his bleeding, semiconscious body.

The three of us laid together for several seconds, our chests heaving, all of us coughing, sweat saturating our fatigues. Beneath us, the kid whimpered and moaned as blood streamed from his nose and mouth. After two minutes passed, or maybe twenty, Brett sat up and removed a plastic handcuff strip from his pants pocket. I feebly restrained the man's legs while Brett wrapped the cuff around the kid's ankles, an unnecessary precaution since he was too injured to run anyway.

After he was bound, my partner and I sat in the dirt for a moment, letting our breathing return to normal and looking at our prisoner. "How we going to get him back to the jeep?" I wheezed.

"I've already thought of that," Brett said, struggling to his feet. He staggered over to an old mamasan who had been watching us from a short distance away, as she balanced a long pole across her shoulders, a bucket of water hanging from each end. Brett talked to her for a moment, pointing once toward the prisoner and once toward me. She nodded, lowered the pole from her shoulders to set the buckets on the ground, and then slid the pole away from their handles. She handed it to Brett as he handed her a coin.

"I've rented us a prisoner transport system," he said proudly on his return.

I didn't immediately understand until he ran one end of the pole under the prisoner's plastic ankle cuff and the other through his wrist cuff, slinging him like a slain deer. We lifted the pole, placing an end on each of our shoulders, and began walking down the alley, the prisoner's sagging rear bumping the ground with our every step. The old woman trailed behind us, calling for everyone to look, so that by the time we got back to the street, we had an entourage of twenty chattering Vietnamese.

We carried our prized catch through the traffic jam, which had just unclogged and was moving at a snail's pace. Our jeep, left in the middle of the street, was now causing most of the problems as a myriad of vehicles struggled to maneuver around it, including a large, blue American military bus with a sign over its front window that read "Bien Hoa Airport."

The bus was crowded with freshly arrived American Servicemen from the United States. Their virgin faces pressed against every window, eyes wide as they watched Brett and I carrying the beaten, bleeding prisoner slung from the wooden pole. At first glance, they probably thought we had captured a Viet Cong, but when it was clear that he was an American, their eyes widened even more.

Brett smiled at the gawking faces and nodded toward the prisoner with a bob of his eyebrows. "Welcome to the 'Nam boys," he said. "Don't break the law during your visit."

This time I didn't take my eyes from the kid, who we placed in the backseat, minus the pole but still bound. Brett once again fought us through traffic and eventually to the highway. The prisoner screamed and cursed most of the way to Long Binh, and whenever it got too annoying, one of us would reach over our seat, slap his shoulder and tell him to hold it down.

At the jail, a booking sergeant met us outside, looking with mild curiosity at our whimpering injured prisoner. I told the sergeant that the kid had gotten hurt when he fell out of the jeep on an especially sharp curve. The sergeant said, "Yes, that happens quite often. Actually, it happens a lot." Then he winked.

When the prisoner realized he wasn't getting any sympathy, he spat a glob on the big man's chest followed with a curse at the sergeant's mother. This was not a wise decision by the kid, since Long Binh jailers didn't treat disrespectful prisoners as nicely as Brett and I.

In a flash, the big sergeant grabbed one of the prisoner's feet and yanked him out of the jeep, his butt and head hitting the ground with a sickening *whump!* A second jailer suddenly appeared and began kicking the prisoner as the booking sergeant drug him by his feet through a door and into a holding cell.

A couple of hours later, we were on the highway again heading back to Saigon. It was a peaceful ride and we even stopped for a while to watch an old farmer plow a rice paddy with his water buffalo. As I gazed at the serene scene, I thought about stories I'd heard of American helicopters flying over Vietnamese farmland as the door gunner, just for giggles, gunned down farmers' water buffaloes.

I recalled a boot camp drill sergeant saying once that the most vicious person in the world was a nineteen-year-old American soldier in Vietnam with an M-16. Judging by what I did and saw others do, there was much truth to his words.

The question that has to be asked is this: Did Vietnam cause it or was it there all along? My experiences in Vietnam taught me that viciousness is part of an uncontrolled warrior spirit, and the horror of such a place can act as a catalyst with some people to bring its ugliness to the surface. While war brings out the best and the worst in us, it also brings out the best and worst of one's warrior spirit.

I'd like to think that today, three decades after Vietnam, I could experience such a place with control and humaneness. Of course, the chance of my ever finding out is slim to none at my age. So I can just kick back and tell myself that those days were another time and another place.

And that I've changed.

THE PEEPER

It was 11 p.m. and I was sprawled in my favorite chair watching the late news and fighting sleep. I must have dozed for a moment because a noise from the kitchen caused me to jump. It was impossible for someone to get into my house, but my imagination and sleepy brain were working overtime. I shook the fuzzies out of my head, walked cautiously to the doorway and peeked slowly around the corner.

Light from the living room partially lit the kitchen — an empty kitchen — just as the logical part of my brain already knew. No burglar, no ghost, not even a boogeyman. Strange though, because there had definitely been a noise and —

A face at the kitchen window.

Again I jumped and a flood of flight-or-fight adrenaline charged through me. I focused harder at the window. The face was still there; its nose, cheek and part of its chin flattened grotesquely against the glass. Then it was gone.

My adrenaline boiled to a rage. As a cop I dealt with street scum every day, but my house was my sanctuary; I was not about to tolerate an intrusion. "Not here!" I shouted, scrambling for my truck keys and gun. "Not here." I jammed the pistol into my waistband and charged out the door, looking left and right.

There! In front of the neighbor's house: a man hopping onto a bicycle. He looked back over his shoulder at me and then pushed off, peddling madly in the opposite direction. I jumped into my truck, spun my tires backwards out of the driveway, then spun them again as I accelerated in the direction I had last seen the peeper. I wanted a piece of this pervert...no, I wanted several pieces. I spotted him passing under a street light about a block away, peddling in obvious desperation. I stomped the accelerator until I was aside him and our eyes met. His face looked terrified, while mine, I'm sure, looked carnivorous.

I goosed the truck ahead of him a little and then made an abrupt turn onto a driveway directly in his path, anchoring my truck just inches from the homeowner's car. The peeper hammered his brakes, sliding his bicycle sideways to a stop a couple of inches from my fender. Before he could right himself, I leapt from my truck and stomped toward him. "What were you doing at my house, pervert?" I growled.

Close up, I was surprised to see that he wasn't a man but a pimply-faced kid, maybe eighteen or nineteen. He looked frightened, but he still made an attempt at some bravado. "Hey man," he sneered with a thrust of his chin. "I don't know what you're talking about."

I hate defiance, especially from someone who has just wronged me by intruding in my personal space. I translated his words as, "What are you going to do about it? I can do whatever I want and you can't stop me."

That pushed my button. As if it had a mind of its own, my hand lashed out and slammed a chop just below his ear. I didn't think it landed that hard, but the kid executed a near-perfect cartwheel off his bike, landing on his back. I was on him in a flash, straddling his chest and pushing the barrel of my pistol into the corner of his trembling lips.

His bravado gone, he tried desperately to scoot away but my weight held him down. "Ple...please don't shoot me," he begged, turning his head to the side and scrunching his face in anticipation of the explosion. "Please...please...."

I had no intention of shooting him, of course, but I did want to make him fill his shorts. "I oughta blow your face off," I said, using my best Clint Eastwood voice.

He stopped begging and turned his head back toward me, his eyes crossing as he looked down the barrel. He looked at me and then down the barrel again, where his eyes remained for a long, silent moment. And then he screamed, an ear-piercing, feminine, gosh-awful scream.

"Hey, cool it," I yelled.

He did, turning it off like a water faucet, but only for a moment. Then he shouted, "Help! Police! Police!"

Feeling I had made my impression, I removed my gun from his lips and slipped it into my waistband. "I *am* the police," I said matter-of-factly. Again he did his bugged eye thing.

"You...?"

"Yep, I'm the man," I said, applying a painful wristlock that forced him over onto his stomach.

Several porch lights came on, and the homeowner of the property on which the peeper and I were sharing a moment opened his door. "Hey, what's going on?" he called, sounding a little frightened. "What are you doing in my yard?" I called out for him to phone the police and to tell them that an off-duty officer had a prowler in custody.

"And tell them to hurry," the kid yelled, his voice somewhat muffled because his face was pressed into the lawn. "This psycho cop is breaking my arm."

As it turned out, someone had already called and a moment later a police car rounded the corner. The officer knew the kid as a peeper and an active burglar in the neighborhood. I had him arrested and he was taken to the juvenile detention center.

Later, as I lay in bed hashing over the incident and trying to will the adrenaline from my muscles, Ol' Mr. Guilt came a visiting.

I had hurt and scared the kid partly because he had trespassed on my property, but mostly because he had frightened me and made me feel vulnerable in my private space. My warrior spirit had kicked in at full throttle when I saw him through my window, and I lost control. I bullied him, violated my principles as a martial artist and my responsibility with a firearm.

Hurting and scaring the kid gave me a moment of satisfaction, but I still felt violated hours later. Bullying him hadn't rid me of that feeling but instead had given me one more to deal with.

Shame.

JAIL

We had arrested an American serviceman in a small alleyway off a main street in Saigon, right after he had exchanged his money for heroin with an old woman, unaware that my two partners and I were watching from a few feet away.

When he saw us moving his way, he tried to rush past us but the alleyway was small and damp, and he slipped on the wet bricks, landing on his belly right at our feet. He was a big man and put up a good fight before we got him under control and handcuffed. Even then, he continued to thrash around as we half-walked and half-carried him back to our jeep.

Each week, my partners and I arrested about a half-dozen American servicemen in Saigon's back alleys who were AWOL, Absent Without Leave, from their units. They would flee to Saigon and live with other AWOLs or with Vietnamese girls. Though most were caught within a couple of months, some managed to hide out for a year or more. We caught one who had been AWOL for more than six years and had fathered two children by his Vietnamese girlfriend. The entire year I worked in Saigon as a military policeman, the AWOL list never had fewer than 1,800 names.

Once we got him into the jeep, he stopped squirming and begrudgingly gave his name as Johnson. I drove and my two partners held onto him tightly in the back seat as his eyes darted around searching for an opportunity to escape. He remained quiet for most of the trip, but he began cursing and thrashing around about a block away from the jail compound. My partners weren't about to let him escape and to make double sure of it, they forced him onto the floor and sat on him.

At the jail, the three of us wrestled Johnson up a flight of stairs to the booking area on the second floor, and then forced him down on a long bench below a large open window. After a couple of minutes, he stopped resisting, but then spat at us and threatened to kill all of us. Once my partners had him under control, I stepped over to the sergeant's desk to explain what was going on.

The booking area was cramped, poorly lit and, because it was on the second floor, oppressively hot and humid. The sergeant's desk was on a raised platform, enabling him to peer down at the prisoners, giving him some psychological intimidation, though it didn't work on every prisoner. A railing, looking something like an iron hitching post, stretched along the front of the desk, about ten feet from the bench where Johnson, now quiet, sat glaring at my partners.

It was the sergeant's job to learn the prisoner's name, the name of his unit and then make contact with the man's commander. Since Johnson seemed to have mellowed out, I relaxed a little and leaned against the railing to tell the sergeant the particulars of the arrest. I was just about to tell him about the heroin when there was a sudden commotion behind me.

I twisted around to see one of my partners stumble away from the bench clutching his bleeding nose, as my other partner drew his wooden nightstick and moved to block Johnson from fleeing toward the door. Behind me, the sergeant screamed for him to sit down. Instead, Johnson turned toward me, curled his lips back like a mad pit bull, crouched and sprang.

His attack was so fast and explosive that I only had time to brace myself against the railing and drive my size-eleven army boot hard into his midsection. It caught him just right because Johnson belched a loud "oomph!" and stumbled backwards, his butt leading the way, arms flailing. The back of his knees struck the bench first, tripping and launching him over the back of it, and then over the low Vietnamese windowsill, out into space.

For the first time since the attack, the desk sergeant stopped yelling. Except for a buzzing fly, the room fell eerily silent as all of us stood frozen, mouths agape, all staring in shock at the open window.

"Where'd he go?" the sergeant bellowed, vaulting over his desk. His loud voice snapped us from our trances and sent us scrambling toward the window.

Two stories down, Johnson lay on his back draped over a sticker bush. We looked down at him and he looked up at us, then we all looked at each other. "Let's get him!" the sergeant barked, again breaking the moment; he led the way to the stairs.

Untangled from the sticker bush, Johnson was much quieter and more cooperative. He complained about where I had kicked him in his stomach, and he had lots of abrasions on his arms and face from the brush. We carried him back upstairs and laid him on a cot in a cell where he moaned for a while before falling asleep.

If there were a moral to be learned here, it would be this: Short-term goals are sometimes formed quickly in the heat of a fight. It's important, therefore, to keep in mind that if the goal is also a shortsighted one, someone might take a nasty fall, like out a window.

CHAPTER TWO
Pieces of Humble Pie

A slice of humble pie is a good thing to eat from time to time, especially for people who, as my mother use to say, "Have gotten too big for their britches." Over the years, I have eaten a lot of slices, and it has always been fed to me at a time when I needed it most, at a time when I was, well, getting too big for my britches. Here are a couple of short examples.

I went to a tournament shortly after I earned my second degree black belt, partly to prance around and be seen wearing the new slash on my black belt, and also to participate in a school-team match that was open to all belt ranks. All my prancing came to an abrupt halt when a colored belt, with less than a year's training, soundly and painfully defeated me in my first fight. He was a Golden Gloves boxer, too, with a punch that nearly shattered my ribs and left a bruise that remained for weeks.

Another example occurred shortly after I had been appointed as a defensive tactics instructor for the Portland Police Bureau's police academy. I was on patrol one day when dispatch sent me to back up a pair of recently graduated rookies needing help putting a grizzled old drunk into the backseat of their police car. When I got there, I gave them a reassuring smile as I got out of my car, as if to say, "Don't worry, I'm here." I may have even given them a patronizing wink.

They said that the old guy wasn't actually fighting them, only balking about getting into the car. I told them that this was a perfect situation to apply thumb pressure to a nerve point on the neck, a technique I had taught them in the academy. It was guaranteed to make the old drunk get into the police car.

I stepped confidently up to the man, who was swaying on his feet and looking dumbly at me, and applied the pressure-point technique. He didn't react. So I pressed harder, but still no reaction. When I pushed hard enough to poke a hole in him, he smiled drunkenly and slurred, "Ain't workin', is it kid?"

Now that I'm older and supposedly wiser, I don't eat as much humble pie as I used to. I'm sure, though, there are still a few pieces waiting for me somewhere, and though I don't like the way they are served, let alone how they taste, I know they are good to eat once in a while.

THE HEIST

Right after I had passed all the tests to be a Portland Police Officer, I was told that due to budget problems there would be a twelve-month hiring freeze. To bide my time and get some practice in police work and real-life application of my martial arts, I took a job as a department store detective in a rough neighborhood. I was training hard for my second-degree black belt, and I felt confident that I could handle anything that came my way.

I spent my shift behind a two-way mirror watching shoplifters hide merchandise in their clothing or shopping bags, and then head to the door without paying. My job was to follow them out, identify myself, escort them back to my office and then call the police. After a couple of months, I had arrested several thieves, mostly kids and elderly women.

It was 1971, and there was a lot of hype about the martial arts, which was growing in popularity every day. The imported Hong Kong kung-fu movies had just hit our shores, and though we laugh at them now, in the early days of karate in the United States, we loved them and identified with the heroes. We knew their three-story leaps and their invincibility against large numbers of attackers were the stuff of corny fiction, but we also wanted to believe that maybe we had some of their awesome powers. There were not as many people studying the martial arts as there are today, so the movies made us unique and mysterious, a reputation we fully enjoyed.

One day I was watching shoppers through the mirror when my attention was drawn to a skinny guy wearing a black leather jacket. He was trying too hard to act casual and nonchalant, and though he thought he was being clever, his actions were as apparent as if he were crying out, "Hello. I'm your shoplifter."

He strolled over to the stereo component display and pretended to read a few labels. He held his head down, but I could still see his eyes darting about like those of a nervous animal. Then in a quick move that I nearly missed, he scooped up a stereo receiver, slipped it under his jacket and headed for the door.

A moment later, I was on his heels. The instant his first foot hit the sidewalk, which made his theft official, I stepped in front of him, identified myself as store security, and told him to come back inside. He gave me a slow, measured look, and then without a word, pulled the stereo receiver out from under his jacket, laid it on the sidewalk and walked casually away as if I didn't exist.

I did exist, though, and to prove it, I grabbed him by the shoulders of his jacket and pulled him back toward me. His jacket came, but he didn't, because in one swift movement he slipped his arms out of his sleeves, leaving me holding the garment as if I were his personal valet.

I tossed it aside and reached for his arm, but something, from somewhere slammed into my jaw, sending me butt-first onto the sidewalk and then over onto my back. I hadn't a clue what had happened, as I struggled up onto one elbow and shake my head to push away the fog.

The first thing that came into focus was the thief, casually picking up his jacket and speaking to another man, whose eyes were focused on me as he held up his fists like a boxer. Now I understood: I had been blind sided, sucker punched. I stumbled to my feet as the man boxer-danced toward me then I stepped back to create a little space between us. Just as he danced into range, I whipped a roundhouse kick toward his groin, hoping to nip his career as an accomplice, not to mention any plans he had for Saturday night. He was fast, though, twisting away so that my foot landed against his hip. I hesitated, expecting him to fall from my killer kick…but he didn't. Instead, he turned and ran off.

Blood trickled down my chin, as my lower lip inflated and my ego deflated. I was suddenly aware of people standing around me, and I heard kids laughing. I picked up the stereo receiver and walked into store, ignoring all the clerks asking if I was okay.

For the next two days, I replayed the confrontation over and over in my mind. Seven years of karate training and I got sucker punched like a white belt novice. Then when I did get a shot at one of the guys, he simply turned away so that my kick missed its intended target, something that never ever happened to the heroes in the kung fu movies. I couldn't understand it.

Maybe my karate instructor could make sense out of it. In a voice that probably sounded like a little boy whining about a big kid taking his ball, I told him what had happened. I sniveled that I just couldn't understand it, me being a black belt and all.

When I finished, my instructor shook his head, not with empathy, but with disgust. "Who do you think you are?" he spat. "Superman? You can't block what you can't see. Your knowledge only gives you an edge, and that's all. Real life isn't a kung fu movie. No matter how good you get or how big you get, there will always be someone out there who can sucker punch you. Sometimes, knowing karate means that you have elevated yourself only to the level of a good street fighter, a guy who has never had a lesson, but has learned on the streets."

He paused for a moment and when he spoke again his voice had softened and his disgust was gone. "Karate is like life: You get ahead and then you get knocked back. You take two steps forward and you get knocked back three. What's important is that you keep trying to do your best. That's part of what being a warrior is all about."

I don't know what I expected from my teacher, but his words brought me back to Earth. I had been living in a fantasy world where I thought I was an unbeatable, invulnerable character in a movie. My sore butt, swollen lip, wilting ego, and his words showed me how wrong I had been. I might have been close physically to getting my second black belt, but I still had a long ways to go as a martial artist.

Since then, I have been hit by surprise a couple of times, but those only hurt my body, not my ego. Today, I accept the fact that my knowledge, training and credentials may give me an edge, but there are still lots of people out there who can knock me on my butt.

THE HURRICANE

In 1968 I was stationed on an army missile base, deep in the jungle of the Florida Everglades. It was an immensely unpleasant place, a hellish brew of wet, oppressive heat, a riot of every creepy-crawly insect known to man, and a plethora of snakes and alligators. I hated being there with a passion, except for the tropical storms. Those I loved.

The frequent bouts of thunder and lightning were so violent that the first time I experienced one I feared it was the end of world. Lightning illuminated the night as brightly as the noon hour and thunder slammed so loudly and with such force that I often thought my chest would be crushed. Horrendous rain pounded and washed away the land, and palm trees, their roots loosened from the deluge, toppled to the ground.

There were lots of stories in Florida about hurricanes, especially the big one that hit in the early 1960s, leaving in its wake destroyed bridges and roads under water. Whenever the locals spoke of it, their voices still trembled from the memory and with dread that there would be another.

I was lying on my bunk one early morning when the company clerk burst into the sleeping bay and announced that a hurricane was going to hit the Florida Keys in a few hours. The company commander wanted all of us up to make preparations.

We took down the television antennae and the flags, brought in the garbage cans, boarded up the windows, tightened this and tied down that. There were sixty of us in the unit and none of us had been in a hurricane before, so we were excited and a little apprehensive about the prospect of getting to experience one in a few hours.

Throughout the morning, not a palm leaf fluttered, and even the surrounding jungle with its billions of creepy crawly inhabitants was soundless. After we had tied down everything, we sat outside, smoked, drank soft drinks and watched the sky turn from tropic blue to dirty yellow. By mid-afternoon it began to get windy.

I was twenty-one-years old in 1968, and I had been training in karate for about four years. Much of my off-duty time was spent practicing and reading magazines and books on the martial arts. Of particular interest was a story about Gichin Funakoshi, the man instrumental in bringing karate to Japan from Okinawa in 1930. One time, during a typhoon in Japan, Funakoshi climbed on a roof to face the full fury of the storm. He assumed a karate stance known for its stability and held it while the violent winds whipped his body. His followers saw the act as a great test of courage, mental discipline and physical strength.

I loved the story and thought about it while awaiting the storm. Funakoshi's stance was not in my karate style, but I did use a strong one called "horse," assumed by placing the feet wider than shoulder-width and squatting down as if sitting on a short, fat horse. The back is held straight and the arms are folded across the chest. It's a great leg-strengthening exercise that when held for thirty minutes or longer tests the discipline of even the toughest martial artist. I decided to pit my horse stance against the storm, just as Funakoshi had.

I told a couple of my buddies about my plan and they looked at me as if I had been kicked in the noggin. In short, they thought it was stupid. I didn't care what they thought, though, because I thought the idea was exotic and very Asianish. I wasn't sure what exotic and being Asianish had to do with standing in a storm, but that's how I saw it in 1968.

Hell broke loose at five p.m. The wind slapped into the side of our brick living quarters like a monstrous, invisible hand, and then it slapped again, its fingers ripping off shutters, breaking glass and pulling away sections of roofing. Torrential rains poured through broken windows and gaping holes in the ceiling. Limbs, vines, moss and giant leaves ripped loose from the jungle and rode on currents of screaming wind until they slammed into the side of our barracks.

Twenty minutes into the storm, the sixty of us had gathered in a long, windowless L-shaped hallway. The electricity had died after the first strong gust, so we sat in darkness making nervous jokes, even after part of the roof disappeared, leaving us sitting under a small waterfall. A sergeant succeeded at frightening us with a story of the Big One that had killed dozens of people five years earlier.

The hallway in which we sat stretched for one hundred feet before making a ninety-degree turn at one end and continuing for about thirty feet before it ended at a door that led outside. No one sat in the short section because the wind had blown out the window of the door, scattering glass the entire length of the hallway. While everyone listened to a guy telling a joke, I stepped around the corner, quickly pulled off my fatigue shirt, took in a deep breath for courage, and slipped out the backdoor right into the belly of the beast.

At first I couldn't move, so strong was the wind pressing me against the side of the building. After a few moments of struggling, I discovered that although literally pinned against the wall, I could, with effort, inch sideways. That worked until I stepped into the open, away from the wall that had been protecting me from the full force of the wind. As if infuriated that I dare challenge it, a mighty gust slapped against my body, sending me head over heels along jagged coral. I managed to grab the trunk of a palm tree and held on as if it were a life preserver, which it was. My bare upper body stung from dozens of small cuts made by the razor sharp coral.

The roar of the rain and wind was far greater than any one beast could make; I had to be in the bowels of hell, and I was in it by my own choice! I managed to climb to my feet between gusts, but the rain and wind, as forceful as a full blast from a fireman's hose, forced my eyes shut. I couldn't see anything. Still, my intention was strong, and I was going to do what I came out to do.

I faced directly into the howling winds and assumed the horse stance, squatting low for strength and stability and leaning forward a little to resist the rage of wind. I was doing it! Mother Nature and I were head to head and I was standing up to her. Ha! This was so cool. I held my head high and let the wind assault me.

Five seconds later, a powerful gust uprooted me, slammed me hard onto my back and sent me rolling on the coral for the second painful time. More terrible than the pain was the sense of total helplessness against the powerful, invisible force rolling me along the ground. I managed to get up between gusts, and opened my watering eyes just long enough to see a large tree branch fly by and ram into an outbuilding, punching a hole into its heavy metal door. This was insane. I had to get back to the barracks.

It took an eternity of falling down, rolling and struggling back to my feet, but I finally made it to the door, which took every ounce of muscle to open and squeeze through. I picked up my shirt from where it lay in a puddle, slipped it on and limped back to the other hallway, where I slid down a wet wall and sat among pieces of roofing. Thankfully, no one paid attention to me. When the storm died a couple of hours later, we set about cleaning up.

Later that night, I lay hurting and exhausted in my bunk trying to make sense out of what I had done. I wasn't sure what I was supposed to have felt, but for sure I didn't feel anything exotic and I didn't feel at all Asianish, whatever that was supposed to mean. I was able to achieve my goal and assume the horse stance, but only because the wind's intensity had died momentarily. But when the next blast came, I went a tumbling. If there was something exotic about that, it was lost on me.

My four years of karate training had only been in physical technique; we were never taught the mental and spiritual benefits. I wasn't even sure what those things were, but for sure I knew that my body hurt and would be hurting even more tomorrow. I was lucky I hadn't been killed, especially when we learned the next day that several people in the Florida Keys had lost their lives to the storm, no doubt trying to save their homes or loved ones.

In 1968, I didn't know a thing about the discipline and courage that Funakoshi had called upon to confront his storm. Since I lacked the self-knowledge he had, I confronted mine with ignorance, a childish fantasy, and without comprehension of the reality of nature's immense power and fury.

I learned that day that while you don't always know your opponent, you had better know yourself.

THE MISS

My partner, Neil, and I were patrolling the north side of Portland, an area the police called "The Avenue." The nickname was short for Union Avenue, a four-lane street that sliced through a run-down business and residential section. It was a scorcher of an August afternoon; in fact, the sun had been frying us the entire week. My partner and I were wilted and short-tempered, and so were the people living and working in the area.

Just as we were about to call it a day and head back to the station, dispatch gave us a call regarding several people fighting in the street. In essence, the call was this: Family A was mad at Family B's dog for leaving little goodies in family A's yard. Now, both families were brawling and more people from both clans were arriving in cars.

Three other police cars were dispatched to back us up, but we were the first to arrive, right in the middle of two-dozen people screaming, pushing and punching each other. Some were fighting on the sidewalk, some in the street and a few were trampling a gorgeous flowerbed in their attempt to get at each other. A big, brown, ratty-looking dog, sat dumbly next to a rhododendron, watching all the mayhem he had started.

Riotous situations were always confusing. Many times when we got to one, it was unclear who were the good guys and who were the bad. We would first separate the players to get some control of the situation and then find out what was going on. That was Neil's and my plan at this one.

We jumped out of the car yelling, "Freeze!" and "Police!" and "Hold it!" but no one in the scattered groups of brawlers acknowledged us. There were two men swinging wildly at one another next to our car, so I jumped into the middle of them. I grabbed one guy's arm to pull him away, but that only made it convenient for the other guy to punch my guy in his forehead. I let go of his arm so he could moan and rub his head, and then I lunged at the one who had hit him. As I struggled to restrain that guy, the one with the sore forehead kicked him in the groin, no doubt thankful for my "help." As my guy moaned loudly and slumped in my arms, I saw Neil rolling on the ground with two heavyset women who were clearly getting the best of him. I lowered my guy to the sidewalk, figuring he wasn't going anywhere anyway, and dashed over to help Neil.

On the way, I saw a guy with a two-by-four board, cocking it back like a baseball player on the mound, running toward another man whose back was turned. I had to make a split-second decision: Save Neil from the fat women or save the guy from getting hit with the board. Although Neil might not have agreed, I chose the citizen and jumped in front of the "baseball player."

As far as timing goes, I should have waited two more seconds, because just as I lunged in, the board whacked full force into my right biceps muscle. The blow was clearly not intended for me; I was just the dummy who got in the way. I looked at the guy with the board and he looked at me. He must have thought, "What the heck. I already hit him once, so I may as well hit him again." He cocked the board back over his shoulder.

No way I was going to let him do that again. Clearly, it was time to clobber him with the very much-dreaded "Loren W. Christensen punch from Hell."

I started my fist way down behind me, like a baseball pitcher winding up a fastball, and launched it with all the mind boggling power and speed I, or any mortal, could muster. If my punch were being filmed for a movie, it would be shown traveling in slow motion, accompanied by eerie music and an expression of absolute horror on the face of the intended victim. Everyone around us would stop and look in our direction, frozen with fear and full of pity for the guy with the board. The tension would be palpable as the punch got closer and closer to the poor sap whose face would soon be in the ozone.

In reality, my punch missed the guy by a mile.

My arm extended impotently in the hot, summer air, probably for no more than a quarter of a second, though it seemed like a full minute. I will never know if the guy saw it coming and moved aside, or if I simply aimed wrong. In either case, he decided to drop the board and make a hasty escape.

With the help of our back-up officers, we eventually calmed the crowd and got everyone heading back to their homes. Two small children led off the smiling dog, but not before he stopped to water a shrub in the same yard in which he had dropped his earlier goodies. The mutt's slap-in-the-face could have caused another riot, but luckily the homeowners didn't see him.

As I rubbed my sore arm, still mortified about the missed punch, my partner walked up brushing dirt from his uniform. There was no way I was going to tell him what happened, and I certainly wasn't going to mention it to anyone else. It wasn't until we started walking toward our car that I noticed the six back-up officers standing next to it, some with their arms folded, all smiling at me.

"Hey Bruce Lee," one of them said. "Nice punch."

All six of them sputtered and laughed as if they had been holding it in too long. Ambling back to their cars and still laughing, a couple of them threw wild punches in the air. "Did you see Loren *Lee* punch that mosquito that was bothering that guy with the board?" one of them asked.

"Yes. He's always so considerate."

"That was ka-ra-te," another said, dissecting the word with sarcasm. "He was doing ka-ra-te on the guy's face."

"Yeah, but too bad his ka-ra-te fist was nowhere near the guy's face."

"Hey guys," I called after them as they climbed into their cars. "Can't this be our little secret?" Their giggling remained in my ears long after they had driven off.

Neil, who I know was too busy to see my miss, was still chuckling at the others as we got into our car. "What happened, anyway?"

I let out a stream of air and felt my shoulders sag. At that time, I had been training in karate for thirteen years; I had earned a second-degree black belt and was sort of a local big shot after winning several tournaments. Missing with the punch was mortifying, but I was confident that Neil wouldn't tease me since he had heard enough of my karate stories to know that sometimes things just happen. "Well, the guy hit me with a board," I said, "and when he tried a second time, I threw a big punch that missed."

He didn't say anything for a long moment, and then, "Maybe you would have better luck defending yourself against a board with a saw."

I shook my head with resignation and scooted low in the seat as Neil pulled away from the curb. I looked out the window, rubbed my arm and chuckled.

There is nothing like looking like a fool to humble a big shot.

WEAK JAW

I was stationed for a few weeks at Lackland Air Force base in Texas. Although I was in the army, Lackland Air Force Base had a sentry dog school that was attended by the Army military police, the Air Force police and the Marine Corps infantry. After completing the nine-week course, the new dog handlers would fly back to their units for duty with their four-legged partners.

My class consisted of about twenty-five men, some veterans, some with just a few months in their particular branch of the military. The training was tough, mostly due to the desert weather that fluctuated from oppressive heat to bone-numbing ice storms. We made the best of it, as people in the military always do, and we all became good, situational friends.

Everyone had a nickname. I was "Karate Killer;" "Bear" was a big marine; an odd, little Air Force man was called "Iggy;" a muscular guy from Georgia was "Sampson;" and "Chief" was from a North Dakota Indian reservation. I'm ashamed to admit it, but I gave "Weak Jaw" his name.

He was from somewhere in the Midwest, about twenty-two years old, tall, skinny and completely void of a jaw. His neck began just below his lower lip and sloped downward to a huge Adam's apple that jutted out as if struggling to escape. When Weak Jaw spoke, that Adam's apple bobbled so insanely that it was hard not to stare.

People with red hair are said to have tempers, people with narrow foreheads are supposed to be stupid, and people with little or no jaws are believed to be cowards. These are old stereotypes that are considered gospel by many. Ridiculous? Of course, but then so are all stereotypes.

I was twenty-one years old, and though I had a big forehead I was in many ways stupid, such as believing the stereotype about jaws. Not only did I believe it, I told others about it, and within a week everyone was convinced that the skinny man from the Midwest was a coward and would be afraid of his dog. Unfortunately for him, I was right. Whether it was a coincidence or a stereotype he fulfilled, Weak Jaw turned out to be deathly afraid of his German Shepard.

Actually, everyone was at least a little afraid when they first met their dogs because most of them were vicious in the extreme. After mine had killed an elderly man in Chicago, the owner gave him to the Air Force to avoid being forced to destroy the dog. It took all of us several days to break down the cautious barrier, but by the end of our second week together, a bond began to form between men and beasts and the mutual fear turned to respect and love.

Weak Jaw, however, remained terrified of his dog, which made the drill sergeants scream and threaten to fail him. At the end of each training day, he was the butt of all the teasing and practical jokes in the barracks, the worst of it coming from me. To get even more laughs, I threw occasional punches and kicks at him, deliberately missing by a fraction of an inch, but coming close enough to startle him. The harassment never let up, but Weak Jaw tolerated it without a word of complaint and even pretended to have fun with it.

The fun of teasing him dimmed during the last couple of weeks, in part because of stress from intensified training, but mostly because Weak Jaw was becoming competent as a dog handler. While most of the guys had accepted him as a peer, I continued to try to get laughs at his expense.

One night during the last week of training, five of us decided to walk to an ice cream stand a few blocks away. As we made our way along the dark street, we joked and poked and carried on, as young men are apt to do. I teased Weak Jaw as usual and, as usual, he took it well. At one point, for no other reason than to get a laugh, I launched a high roundhouse kick from behind him, intending to stop it just short of his ear. But just as my combat boot completed its arc and was about a half a foot from his head, Weak Jaw spun around and caught my leg in the crook of his arm.

Time stood still. Our eyes locked as we both contemplated the full impact of our new status: his one of power, mine of extreme vulnerability. Weak Jaw smiled, the way a father will smile as he is about to let his son error to teach him a lesson.

Without changing his expression, he pushed my leg upward, sending me backward into a flapping, floating descent that seemed to last forever. Before I landed, I caught just a glimpse of the other guys' open mouths, and then my back went ku-*plump!* onto the pavement, knocking out my wind, along with my ego.

Faces looked down at me with a mix of shock and concern. "You okay?" someone finally asked. The asphalt felt cold and hard, and though my wind was gone and my back hurt, I scrambled to my feet and straightened my army fatigues with as much dignity as I could muster.

Seeing that I wasn't hurt, the guys began laughing and slapping Weak Jaw's back. In a quick second, the dynamics of our group had changed. "Hey," one of them said, laughing. "Maybe we should change the names here." He squeezed Weak Jaw's shoulder affectionately. "You are now Karate Killer. And Christensen, you're Weak Jaw."

Everyone laughed and resumed walking toward the ice cream stand, reliving what had just occurred and congratulating the new Karate Killer about his cool technique. I trailed a few feet behind them, a little embarrassed and a whole lot humbled. I knew in my mind that I had not thrown the kick as fast as I could, but that was hardly the point. I had kicked at him to get a laugh at his expense, regardless of how it made him feel. This time, though, the roles reversed, and I became the joke.

Maybe it was the skull-rattling fall that knocked some sense in my head, because suddenly I saw everything differently. Since I had passed judgment that Weak Jaw was weak, I had been teasing him incessantly for weeks. The reality, however, is that he had shown extraordinary courage and was as tough as the rest of us, maybe more. Although fearful of his dog, he had faced him every day until he conquered his fear. I wondered if I could have done as well had my dog been especially vicious or if I had been afraid of him for whatever reason. Weak Jaw also faced merciless teasing without ever uttering a complaint. I hadn't liked even the minor teasing I had just gotten after being dumped onto my back. Could I have handled it day after day as he had?

As we continued our walk, Weak Jaw reacted no more to the compliments and praises from the guys than he had to the earlier teasing. When we were about a block from the ice cream stand, he held back to wait for me to catch up. "Are you all right?" he asked with genuine concern.

I smiled and nodded. "Yes, thank you, Karate Killer."

He looked at the others who were several yards in front of us. "You can call me Mike if you want."

I held his eyes for a moment. There was a look of maturity in his face I hadn't noticed before. "Thanks," I said.

"For what?" His eyes revealed that he already knew the answer.

"For teaching me what bravery and strength are all about."

At the ice cream joint, Mike held the door for me. "Let me buy you a cone," he said.

During the last two weeks of training, I called him Mike and he called me Loren.

Everyone else called me Weak Jaw.

SAMPSON

The nighttime dispatcher's monotone voice crackled over the radio: "All units, there's a disturbance at 400 Flowers Street with dozens of GI's and Vietnamese involved. Several are reported to be down and injured."

Flowers Street was in a busy part of Saigon, a street lined with bars, brothels and sidewalks jammed day and night with servicemen, prostitutes, beggars and thieves. Dispatch didn't say what had started the disturbance or what all was involved, but at midnight, we assumed it was a drunken argument over a prostitute, maybe a racial clash or a bad drug deal.

What had been an uneventful shift for us suddenly changed as we rounded a corner from a quiet alleyway onto Flowers Street right smack into the middle of a full-scale riot.

At the epicenter was a guy who looked like Victor Mature in that old biblical movie *Sampson and Delilah* where he uses a jawbone from a mule to club an entire army of Philistines. But this wasn't a movie and the big guy wasn't an actor with a plastic jawbone. He was an American serviceman, big as boxcar, wielding a hammer on a crowded Saigon street. Just like Victor Mature, this Sampson was clubbing everyone in sight and, judging by the number of people on the ground, he had been doing it for several minutes before my partner and I, along with several other MPs, pulled into to the scene. The riot wasn't all about him, though, as there were dozens of others fighting in the street, on the sidewalk and in and out of doorways. My guess was that Sampson and his "jawbone" were responsible for most of those on the ground.

In the next couple of minutes, twenty additional MPs were called. As each unit pulled into the mess, they were instantly thrust into the fray — grabbing people, throwing some to the ground, getting punched and kicked and pursuing people down the streets and sidewalks. From somewhere came a heart-stopping burst from an M-16, scattering some, though in a war-torn city like Saigon, the sound of automatic gunfire had less impact than it would in a crowded street back home.

My partner and I stopped our jeep about fifteen feet behind Sampson. Seeing several bleeding people lying at his feet, I had a fleeting thought about shooting the big guy, but since he was in the midst of dozens of people, a missed shot would continue zinging through the air until someone else stopped it.

I rushed toward him from behind, though not sure what I was going to do when I got there. Sampson decided for me, however, when he cocked back his hammer to clobber a Vietnamese man whose throat he was sqeezing as he dangled him in the air. Without hesitation, I drove my fist into Sampson's spine.

He didn't react, and brought the hammer down onto the man's head with a sickening *Gusshh!* sound. He flung the limp body aside and then looked right and left for another victim. I punched him again in the spine and a second time in the kidney. I hit him with my most powerful punches, hesitating after each one for the monstrous guy to drop, as have all the others I've hit. But Sampson didn't. He didn't even acknowledge me hitting him. Instead, he cocked his hand back ready to clobber someone else with his hammer.

I drove in three more punches, but he ignored those, too, as he brought his hammer down on the head of a previous victim lying at his feet. Again I hit him and again and again. Still he ignored me. Then I drove a hard one into the back of his head, an area vulnerable to even mild impact. That got his attention.

He didn't stagger or fall, but at least he turned around and acknowledged my presence. Just as I was wondering what I was going to do as a follow up, another MP appeared on my right and smashed his pistol into the giant's forehead.

Like a scene out of a bad horror movie, Sampson shook his head and blinked a few times as if to erase the pain, and then he turned to face the MP. Without pause, the MP used his gun again to slam Sampson in the head, while I simultaneously drove in another reverse punch to the back of his head. This time the big guy staggered. We hit him again and again, the blows eventually wilting him down onto his knees. Another MP came up from somewhere and the three of us dived on him, knocking him onto his belly where he struggled for along time before we got the handcuffs on him.

After I got off shift, I thought about Sampson's tolerance to pain as I applied ice to my wrist, swollen and sprained from all the ineffectual blows to his thickly muscled back. My pride hurt too, as it's not just a little ego-deflating to be ignored by someone you are raining your best punches on. Putting all that aside, the experience taught me not to rely on just one punch or kick to end a confrontation. While at times the human body can be quite fragile, there are other times it can tolerate a tremendous amount of punishment. In subsequent physical encounters in my years as a police officer, I found that sometimes a variety of techniques are needed.

It's not always the best plan to rely on just one way to accomplish a task, even if that way has been successful in the past. It's better to have a quick follow-up, a Plan B, for those special times when Plan A isn't enough.

A Plan C is good to have, too.

CHAPTER THREE

Moments in the Sun

"In the future everyone will be famous for fifteen minutes," said the late Andy Warhol.

I have been lucky enough to have enjoyed a few such occasions of what I like to call "moments in the sun," and have found them to be wonderful, intoxicating and dangerously addictive. Having experienced them to a small degree, it's easy to see why movie stars, recording artists, politicians and sports figures reach so hard for great fame and recognition and then fight vigorously, sometimes shamelessly, to hold onto it.

I like the way writer William Faulkner describes fame through his protagonist in *The Reivers*. The young man had just won a horse race and was basking in the loud cheers and applause. He said, "And so I had my moment of glory, that brief, fleeting glory, which of itself cannot last, but while it does, it's the best game of all."

I have had a few other moments in the sun besides the ones I relate here, and like these, they have all been a result of expressing my warrior spirit. Sometimes they lasted only the fifteen minutes Warhol spoke of, while other times they lasted longer. But long or short, they have been permanently recorded in my memory.

Please believe me that my purpose in presenting these stories here is not to boast, but to show yet one more aspect of the warrior spirit. An aspect that is pretty darn cool.

A BRIEF, FLEETING GLORY

It's called kama, and I was attracted to it the first time I saw a picture in a karate magazine of a Japanese master holding one in each hand. A kama is an ancient sickle, consisting of an eight-inch long handle on one end and a curved, razor-sharp blade on the other. Okinawan farmers used it in the seventeenth century to chop down stalks of grain and rice. When Japan conquered the island in 1609 and confiscated all weapons, the farmers were forced to adapt their farm tools to the martial arts. With practice, a farmer-turned-warrior could hold a kama in each hand and easily hack through the soft tissue of a half dozen attacking enemy soldiers.

The magazine displayed a series of photos of the master demonstrating a short kata, a series of defensive and offensive movements against several imaginary opponents. Since I didn't know of a an instructor teaching the kama, I emulated the pictures and taught myself how to use them, first using a pair of twelve-inch sticks and later a pair of razor-sharp sickles purchased from a Japanese gardening store. Once I learned the simple kata in the magazine, I was hungry for something more complex and with a greater degree of difficulty.

I began experimenting with the weapon to learn all of its possibilities, spending exhausting hours in front of a large mirror developing a variety of hacking, twirling, slicing, chopping, crisscrossing and spinning movements, coordinating them with fancy footwork, high jumps and kicks. Since I practiced with sharp blades, I inflicted several cuts on my arms and chest. On a couple of occasions, I stabbed the blades deep into my shins (that really hurts, by the way).

It took twelve months to painstakingly develop a kata with more than one hundred movements. Practicing daily, I was frequently so exhausted that I could barely lift my arms, let alone the weapons. I applied every ounce of my energy to make each movement precise, fast and as explosive as possible.

When I tested for my second-degree black belt, I demonstrated the kata to fulfill a creativity requirement. My instructor liked it and was so pleased that he encouraged me to enter the forms division at the upcoming Northwest Nationals Karate Tournament. I agreed, but with trepidation.

In 1971, no one in the Northwest had seen the kama, so it was impossible to know how other martial artists and the crowd would accept it. What if they hated it? What if they thought the kata and my performance were absurd? To distract me from such negativity, I began training even harder than I had for my belt promotion. Physically, I pushed myself beyond what I thought I was capable of, and I used mental visualization every day to "see" the audience, to "hear" them cheer and to "see" the trophy being handed to me.

When the tournament day finally arrived, I was ready as I would ever be but still worried about how the audience would accept what I had to show them. Although it was a summer tournament, which is usually poorly attended, it turned out to be the biggest of the year, with hundreds of competitors and a huge noisy audience. *Oh good,* I thought, *just what I didn't need my first time out. Why couldn't everyone have gone on a picnic?*

To prepare my muscles and my psyche, I warmed up outside in a secluded part of the college campus, going through the movements several times at medium speed. With just minutes left before the start of my event, I performed the entire kata at full speed.

Maybe it was due to apprehension or a slick section of grass, but when I executed a crisscrossing movement, I brought one of the blades too close to my right hand, slicing it deeply into a large vein across the back of my knuckles. An arc of red splattered my bare feet and white uniform.

I dropped down onto one knee, applying pressure with my other hand against the gash, just as three of my students ran up and said the officials had been calling my name over the intercom because my kata division was about to start. I showed them what had happened and told them I couldn't get the blood to stop arcing. I sent one of them to see if the tournament director could wait a couple of extra minutes, while the two other students and I worked to get the bleeding slowed and a tight bandage applied.

I hurried into the gymnasium seconds before my division was to start and managed to slip quickly into line with the other contestants, just as the head judge signaled for us to bow, signifying the start of the event. Since I had been unavailable to jockey for position during the sign-up, my name had been entered as the last to compete, providing lots of time for the butterfly war inside my stomach to escalate.

The other competitors demonstrated the usual weapons seen in the division: nunchaku, two twelve-inch sticks joined by a chain on one end; bo, a six-foot pole; and sai, two fork-shaped stabbing weapons. All the katas were performed superbly.

When my name was finally called, there was a fleeting moment when I thought my numb legs wouldn't let me step forward. I looked down at fresh blood oozing through my bandage and felt the wound throb under my gaze. *There's nothing like a severed vein to ruin a guy's concentration,* I thought. Then, for a fleeting second, *Hmm. It's not too late to dash across the gym floor and out the door.* Then: *No chicken boy. You're staying and you are going to go out there and do it.*

I forced the pain out of my mind, stepped up sharply before the judges and announced my name, school name and the name of my kata. The head judge nodded, indicating that I was to begin. I bowed again, stepped back a few feet and assumed a position of attention, holding the kamas alongside my legs. The throbbing in my hand had returned, too intense to ignore, and the waiting eyes of the judges sent the warring butterflies in my stomach into battle again. The audience sounded restless, no doubt hot and tired from sitting on the hard bleachers. They didn't know me, but they had just seen the local champions perform excellently, so they were anxious to know which one of them would be the winner.

I closed my eyes and inhaled deeply, drawing in energizing oxygen and a powerful sense of my warrior spirit. I felt it swirl throughout my body as my respiration increased and my muscles began to twitch in anticipation of the impending battle. I was ready, charged, my anxiety gone as was the throbbing in my hand.

I punctuated my first explosive move with an ear-piercing scream, and for effect, I held the dramatic-looking posture for five seconds. Then, like a madman, I began cutting and kicking and twirling and swirling through the kata with every ounce of warrior spirit I could muster. Forgetting the judges, my hand and the crowd, everything came together — stances, thrusts, slices and kicks. I was an incarnate samurai, engaged in battle against a dozen bandits in the hot dust of a mountain village at the foot of Japan's Mt. Fuji.

Two minutes later it was over. I returned to the position of attention from which I began and stood there motionless, sweat streaming into my eyes, lungs burning, and muscles quaking from the exertion. As my fighting spirit dissipated, the college gymnasium and all the people came into focus. That is when I detected the silence that was, to use a cliché — deafening. The butterflies began fighting again. *When would the laughter come?* I thought. *I must have looked like a total idiot.*

Then it began: First, with one person clapping (probably my mother) and then another and another. A moment later, it all broke loose: a thunderstorm of applauding, cheering, whistling and shouting. Thirty seconds into it, the crowd began stomping on the bleachers, a low, rumbling noise at first, building in volume until it became an almost frightening cacophony.

When I tried to leave the arena with the three-foot high, first-place trophy, I was surrounded by hordes of people wanting to see the kama, offering congratulatory slaps on the back and asking for my signature on their programs. Flashbulbs popped in my face and kids tugged at my uniform. The city newspaper interviewed me outside, and a TV news crew filmed me performing the kata again. The clamor never let up until later that evening when I escaped through a side door to the parking lot.

61

Since that day I have captured over 50 wins in tournaments. While it's always fun to win and to get positive audience feedback, the experience of that first win will remain etched in my mind forever. The most cherished part of that memory — and I'm hesitant to admit it — was that delicious moment when I was King For A Day!

It was a marvelous time that I will remember warmly when I'm old and my joints no longer work so well. It's a memory of my moment in the sun, a rich moment of palatable wonder that every person should experience once in his or her lifetime, for at least fifteen minutes.

BAR FUN

Bill, a tall, lean farmer from somewhere in Kansas, had been in Vietnam for almost a year; I had been there for a month. One day we were working day shift, trying hard to coast through the last couple of hours without a problem. We patrolled a busy strip, mostly bars and brothels that were just outside the gates of Tan Son Nhut Air Force Base and within walking distance of several Army, Navy and Marine installations. This meant that from 6 a.m. to 1a.m., the strip was choked with prowling American servicemen. With so many men drinking and interfacing with the opposite sex, the majority of our shift was spent breaking up fights so that the troops would be healthy enough to fight the Vietcong the next day.

I reached for the mike as soon as I heard our number squawked. "Tango Bravo One, you've got a fight at Love's Bar, 1400 Trung Hung Dao Street. There's an off-duty MP involved." Bill was already accelerating toward Love's as I rogered the call and flipped on the siren to help clear a path through the heavy traffic. While we always hurried to fight calls in the event they might escalate to knives or guns, Bill pushed it even harder since one of our own was involved.

"I hope I can use the new Mace my mama sent me from back home," Bill shouted above the wailing siren, sounding like an excited kid talking about a new toy. "It's supposed to be real good tear gas. I just got it at mail call yesterday." Like a lot of guys who had been in Vietnam for a long time, Bill seemed to like the action a little too much.

Love's Bar was on a corner of a dirt-road intersection. Its entire front consisted of a screen to allow in cool air; at the moment, it allowed a crowd to peer in to watch whatever was going on inside. I jumped out before Bill had brought the jeep to a complete stop. "I'm going in," I shouted over my shoulder.

"Wait. I gotta find my ..." was all I heard him say before I pushed my way through the crowd.

I stood in the doorway for a moment to see what was going on inside. Several chairs were overturned and most of the tables had been knocked askew. Against a far wall, a gaggle of Vietnamese bar girls chattered excitedly and clutched one another as "Doc," holding a barstool over his head, stood in the center of the room looking fearfully at three Vietnamese soldiers standing to his left, right and center. Every time one leaped toward him, Doc swung the stool, sometimes hitting a shoulder or an upraised arm, but mostly missing.

Doc wasn't really a doctor, but a hard-drinking MP who had gotten the nickname from somewhere. Sober, he was a nice guy and popular in our unit, but he rarely got through an every-other day drinking binge without getting into a fight with someone, usually a bar girl or a Vietnamese citizen. This time he decided to tackle the Vietnamese army. His shirt was torn and blood trailed from one of his nostrils. Doc had done something to rile the soldiers and they weren't about to back down even when I yelled at them.

The closest one turned toward me and assumed a basic boxer's stance. I don't know why he wanted to pick on me, but there was no time to think about it. His middle was open, so I whipped a hard roundhouse kick into his stomach, which doubled him over and made him choke audibly, while leaving his head exposed. A solid punch to his ear dropped him to the floor where he stayed, curling into a ball and covering his head with one hand.

When the second soldier charged, I held my ground until he was within range and then stopped him dead in his tracks with a sidekick into his ribs. I expected him to fall backwards, but he remained jackknifed over my foot for a two count. When I retracted my leg, he lowered his head, looked down at the dust imprint of my boot on the front of his shirt and tried feebly to wipe it away. I followed with another kick to the same place, harder this time. That one sent him hurtling backwards, crashing to the floor and sliding on his back. I started to move toward him, but stopped when he rolled over and crawled on all fours toward the door.

I spun around to confront the third man. In the corner of my eye I could see that Doc had lowered his stool and moved to stand next to the bargirls. I didn't care that he wasn't helping or that my partner hadn't come in yet because I was having a good time.

The other soldier was reluctant to come forward, so I went to him. He cocked his fist, but I sent mine first into his face, hard. That sent him stumbling backwards through a curtain of beads and down onto the floor. I expected him to jump up and rush back into the room, but after struggling to his feet and palming blood from his lips, he decided to head out the back door.

This was the most fun I'd had in a long time. I looked over at Doc, now sitting on the stool and staring at me with his mouth agape. Just as I started to ask him if he was okay, Bill burst into the bar holding his can of mace in front of him. He looked around the room and then over to me. "Damn-it, Christensen. I told you to wait for me to get my mace."

"Sorry," I said.

A crowd of Vietnamese mobbed Bill and I as we escorted Doc to the jeep. Several of them grabbed my hands and rubbed the calluses on the backs of my knuckles.

"Karate?" some asked. There was a lot of excited whispering that I couldn't understand, except for the word "karate." Hands reached toward me as I climbed into the jeep, some patting my back and others rubbing my knuckles.

"Number one GI!" they said. "Karate number one!"

I shook their hands and nodded acknowledgement at their frantic waves and shouts of goodbye. As we drove off, some of the children ran behind us for a ways.

"I wish you would have waited," Bill complained again. "I couldn't find Mama's mace 'cause it was under all my gear at the very bottom of my duffle bag." He was pouting.

"Sorry," I said for the second time in five minutes, though I really wasn't. I had had a good time during my "fifteen minutes" of being a kung fu hero.

I discovered that day that a battle is more fun when you don't give the enemy a chance to hit back.

FEEL GOOD ABOUT YOUR 15 MINUTES

It's commonly said that a braggart, who tries to convince everyone that he is superior, is really a person who lacks confidence and needs the reassurance of others. If he is truly superior, it would be apparent in his actions and how he makes others feel about themselves. I agree, but I also believe that there is nothing wrong about feeling good about your accomplishments as long as you do it quietly. In fact, I think it's beneficial to your growth as a warrior to feel good about what you have done.

When I was competing in karate tournaments and sporadically winning those big, gaudy trophies, I had a routine that I did for me and also as a way to teach my philosophy to my children. Whenever I returned home from a tournament with a win, I'd set the trophy on the dining room table, right where everyone could see it. For the rest of the day on Saturday and all day on Sunday, I would pass by it and feel good about my accomplishment. "You saw my trophy, right?" I'd jokingly ask my family over and over, to which they would roll their eyes and shake their heads in mock disgust.

By Sunday evening, my period for basking in my accomplishment had come to an end. I'd put the trophy away in an upstairs room, and start thinking about Monday, a new day to strive for new goals.

I no longer compete in karate tournaments, but I still allow myself to feel good about an accomplishment. For example, when a magazine article or a book that I've written has been published, I set it on the dining room table for a couple of days. Every time I walk by, I run my hand over the surface of the publication and feel good about my accomplishment. Two days later, I file it away and get busy on another.

The journey to an accomplishment is often a battle: There are some skirmishes that advance you and some that knock you back. Some engagements you win and some you lose. The size of the battle is unimportant.

Perhaps you have trained hard during your first four months of martial arts training and you've been awarded your first belt. Or maybe you've been training for twenty years and you've been presented with your fifth-degree black. Maybe you have built a cute, little birdhouse for your backyard or you have designed a multimillion-dollar, high-tech hotel/casino in Las Vegas.

Whatever the battle you have won, it's vitally important that you pause for a couple of days and feel good about your accomplishment.

Then get off your butt and move on to the next battle.

CHAPTER FOUR

Revenge and Venting

We could get revenge in sensational ways if there weren't those annoying hindrances called laws, morals and ethics. The inconsiderate owner of that barking dog next door could be taken out with a fragmentation grenade. How about in the parking lot when someone, without apology, bangs his car door against the side of your new one? Wouldn't you love to take a chain saw and cut his car into little pieces, and if he puts up too much of a fuss...

Life is full of owners of barking dogs and inconsiderate car dingers, as well as thoughtless neighbors who play their stereos loudly, bullies who crowd in line, creeps who throw litter in your yard and morons who tell racial jokes. Since we can't satisfy our need for revenge by really blowing them up or hacking them into little pieces with a chain saw, it's possible, if we allow it to happen, for them to frustrate us, anger us and drive us over the edge. Tea kettles whistle when their innards boil, but humans get ulcers, have heart attacks, deliberately ram their cars into crowds, or snipe people from rooftops with high-powered rifles.

I have used my warrior spirit, coupled with my imagination, to give me at least a sense of getting even with some of life's irritants. I've found this to be an effective way to release frustration, irritation and anger, and replace those negative emotions with a sense of control and ultimately a sense of empowerment. When a situation has pushed me to the edge of my tolerance, I visualize that the source of it is in front of me in the air or on the surface of my heavy bag. Then I punch and kick until all my rage, tension and stress have dissipated with my perspiration and rapid breathing, leaving me with a sense of having some empowerment and control over the situation.

If I didn't have karate, I would use a hammer to pound nails, a tennis racket to smash balls or an axe to chop wood. I know I would have to do something because life never eases up, and the rage must be vented.

INTENT

I hated Drill Sergeant Collier, which is why it felt so darn good to kill him. Well, I sort of killed him.

I was twenty-one years old when I went into the Army in 1967, and I had been studying karate for two-and-a-half years. I was a little older than most of the other recruits in basic training, so my age and karate background should have given me a little psychological edge against all the brainwashing that went on over the nine weeks of intense physical and mental training. The reality was that I was just as susceptible to it as were the others, and just as intimidated and frightened, too.

Basic training in the 1960s was hell. It was physically and mentally exhausting, as we were often pushed beyond our physical limitations while being brainwashed into believing that the drill sergeants would beat us and even kill us for the smallest provocation. We were young, away from our homes and loved ones for the first time and under the dictatorship of cruel, sadistic and often stupid men. That made it easy for the drill sergeants to gain complete psychological control over us and convince us that whether we lived or died was totally up to them. They definitely

68

had me. Though I didn't believe they would kill me, I knew they could make my life so miserable that I would want to be dead.

I wasn't a great soldier in boot camp and I wasn't a bad one; I just tried to stay in the middle so as not to be noticed. Nonetheless, I had my turn in the barrel as the victim of concentrated harassment.

Drill Sergeant Collier was the meanest looking son-of-a-bitch I had ever seen, and I must have had a face he didn't like because he made me his pet project on several occasions. He was a black man, well over six feet tall, bulging with two hundred and twenty-five pounds of muscle that threatened to rip through his impeccably starched fatigues with his every move. His face looked like a giant's clenched fist, with a forehead that could easily drive railroad spikes, and large, wet eyes that pierced like a laser. Rumor had it that he had killed lots of Vietcong with his bare hands during his three tours; my guess was that he paralyzed them first with his eyes, and then snapped off their heads.

My first run in with Drill Sergeant Collier was at the firing range on a scorcher of a July day at the end of six-hour shooting session. We had formed a single line of one hundred and fifty men, all of us facing the sun, creeping ever so slowly through the shimmering heat toward the mess tent. Feeding that many recruits meant that if you were as far back in the line as I was that day, you spent an hour standing at parade rest, snapping to attention before taking a single step forward, and then snapping back to parade rest again.

"What you smiling at, boy?" Drill Sergeant Collier boomed like the sound of heavy artillery. Though I couldn't see him from where I was standing at attention and staring straight ahead, I knew in my gut that his question was directed toward me. A moment later I could see him in the corner of my eye, lumbering his Paul Bunyon frame in my direction.

"You!" he screamed, bending forward at the waist so that his nose was an inch from mine. "I'm talking to you, boy. You smiling at me?"

My heart thumped against my throat. "I wasn't smiling, Drill Sergeant," I croaked feebly. If I looked as if I were, it was because I was grimacing into the blazing sun. Of course the sergeant didn't care about my reason because he was just looking for someone to harass. Some drill sergeants harassed us because they were following the Army's plan of breaking us down mentally so they could build us back into warriors. Others did it because they were cruel and stupid bullies. Mostly they did it because in the 1960s they had free reign and no one ever thought about suing or writing their congressman, not that it would have done any good back then.

"You queer for me, boy? You smiling at me 'cause you love me, son?"

"I wasn't smiling, Drill Sergeant." I stood motionless and kept my eyes staring straight ahead. No one else moved either, nor did they make a sound. Not even the birds chirped.

"You calling me a liar, maggot?"

"No Drill Sergeant."

"Then you *was* smiling at me. So you *must* love me."

"No Drill Sergeant. I don't love you."

He was standing so close that the brim of his Smokey the Bear hat touched my forehead. "If you don't love me, son, then you must hate me."

Clearly this was a no-win conversation. I didn't answer him.

"Aren't you talking to me now, boy? You must want to fight Drill Sergeant Collier. That what you want?"

How did he come to that conclusion out of this conversation, I wondered. "No," I said softly, wondering if this would ever end. Sweat streamed into my eyes.

"No? You said no, son? You scared of me, maggot?" He was really enjoying himself now. Nearby, another drill sergeant giggled, the same kind of giggle a mean kid makes as he rips wings from a squirming fly.

"No, Drill Sergeant. I'm not scared of you." Oh man. Why did I say that?

The sergeant stepped back dramatically, a look of surprise and amusement spreading across his face. He wasn't used to such talk from a recruit; usually everyone wilted and wept when they were the targets of his attention. His lips twisted into a contortion that might have been his smile. This was turning out to be more fun than he had planned.

He pulled off his green neck scarf and started unbuttoning his shirt. "We gonna have us some kick-ass fun now, son."

"I don't want to fight you, Drill Sergeant," I said, trying to get myself out of this mess. My stomach was doing a strange flip-flop thing, and I had to go to the latrine.

Collier pulled his shirt out of his fatigue pants, and finished unbuttoning it, revealing a muscle-plated chest and a six-pack of abdominal muscles. "Tell you what, boy. I'll give you a bayonet. That sound fair?" Again his mouth contorted into that ugly smile, though his eyes looked dead, probably like the eyes of all those Vietcong he'd killed.

"I don't need a bayonet," I said. Shéesh! Did that really come out of my mouth? When did I plan to shut up?

Drill Sergeant Collier's "smile" disappeared; he was no longer amused. Not only was he not getting the reaction from me that he wanted, the ball was suddenly in his court. A dumb boot camp recruit had just forced him to react, and that wasn't a smart thing for me to have done.

A runt of a guy we called Mouse stood two or three guys behind me. As the company clown, he was always good for a few wise-ass remarks under his breath while we stood in formation. Sometimes, though, he chose the wrong time to do it, such as this time. "I'll put my money on Christensen," he called out in a deliberate, high-pitched voice. Some in the line snickered, more to break the tension than because the comment was funny.

Instead of laughing, Drill Sergeant Collier lunged toward Mouse and drove his thick index finger into the hollow of the small man's throat. Mouse's head snapped down and an odd, gurgling sound came from his gaping mouth. He began to reach

71

toward his throat, but his legs collapsed from under him and down he went into the dirt.

For a moment, Drill Sergeant Collier towered over the little man, looking down at him as if he were a spat-out wad of chewing tobacco. Then, ever so slowly, he turned toward me, piercing me with those big, wet, VC killing eyes. He didn't say a word, but those eyes conveyed that our moment was far from over. He stormed off and disappeared behind the mess tent.

Several days passed without seeing Drill Sergeant Collier, and I wasn't missing him. Then one morning in the mess hall, while carrying my tray of food to a table, there was a sudden blur of motion to my right. I knew it was the sergeant even before his foot slammed into my tray, sending it flying through the air, showering food over everything and everyone before it clanged off the far wall.

Drill Sergeant Collier's big ugly face suddenly appeared in mine, his breath reeking of last night's beer. "You clumsy today, boy?" he screamed. "Clean up this mess and get the hell out of my mess hall."

For the next few days, he screamed at me whenever he was near. I couldn't do anything right for him, and he took great pleasure in ridiculing me in front of the others. He was loud, obnoxious and he never missed an opportunity to make the other trainees' lives miserable, too.

One day we were on the firing range and the man next to me was having a problem shooting accurately while lying on his stomach. Drill Sergeant Collier screamed and berated him with every epithet in existence, sometimes while straddling him and nudging the man's ribs with his boot. Still, the recruit couldn't shoot to the drill sergeant's satisfaction. Finally, in a fit of rage, the sergeant stepped on the back of his head and stood on it with his full weight, forcing the man's face into the sand. The recruit's screams were muffled and his struggle was ineffective against the bigger man's weight. Drill Sergeant Collier stood on him for several seconds, and then stepped off and casually strolled down the firing line as if nothing had happened.

By now my hatred of the sergeant had superseded my fear of him. I knew I couldn't do anything without getting sent to the stockade or being made to start basic training over again, but I was beginning to wonder if it might be worth it.

Our final training exercise was with our M16 rifles and blank ammunition. We had to advance in rugged terrain about two hundred yards over logs, around trees, into ditches and over small hills. Two of us would run for a short distance and take cover behind a log or large rock and lay down cover fire while the two other guys advanced. Then it was their turn to do it for us. As we progressed across the field, the drill sergeants circulated among the men and made corrections in their movements and tactics.

It was a fun exercise and I was beginning to feel like a real soldier during this last week of training. About halfway through it, I was lying behind a log, my rifle trained on an imaginary enemy, when I saw Drill Sergeant Collier about a hundred feet in front of me. Per his usual, he was screaming at a recruit and striking the man's helmet with a tree branch. Every ounce of hatred I felt for him boiled to the surface; I wanted to kill him and rid the Army of a bully and monster.

There was confusion all around: shouting, yelling and shooting, so no one was looking at me. I looked down the barrel of my M16, pretending as if I were still in the scenario, though I was really looking at the big sergeant in my sites. He looked good there — vulnerable and at my mercy — but I wasn't going to give him any.

I lowered my head a little further down on the weapon, just as Drill Sergeant Collier had taught us, and watched him strut and scream at people, totally oblivious of the attention I was giving him. My finger tightened on the trigger, my breathing quickened, my heart raced. The M-16's sites were centered on his chest, right on his evil heart. Two weeks earlier I had been awarded the army's Expert badge in marksmanship.

I pulled the trigger; the rifle exploded and bucked in my hands. A blotch of red splashed on the sergeant's chest and red sprayed out from his back. His big, wet eyes widened and then squinted as pain, red and hot, scorched through his mean body. He twisted oddly and then toppled backwards, landing heavily across a large rock. One leg quivered, kicked, quivered again, and then went motionless. Forever.

I felt wonderful.

Of course Drill Sergeant Collier hadn't been shot, there was no blood and he didn't fall down. I did pull the trigger but the bullet was a blank. The rest that followed happened only in my imagination, though it was so vivid to me that for an ever-so-brief moment, I really believed that I had killed the bastard. I felt odd: a little guilty and a whole lot liberated.

Drill Sergeant Collier had not even been looking at me, nor was he aware I had "shot" him, but that didn't matter. In my mind, in my heart and with all my intention, I killed him.

An odd, yet pleasant feeling washed over me. Suddenly the sergeant was no longer significant. I was no longer fearful of him, nor did I feel hate for him. I felt nothing. My warrior spirit had been appeased.

For the next few minutes he worked his way up the hill to my position. When he saw me, he stopped for a moment and gazed at me with a little boy's look of wonder on his face.

"Private Christensen," he said in a voice that was ...normal? I wasn't sure since I had never heard him speak that way to anyone.

"Yes, Drill Sergeant," I smiled, looking him straight in the eyes.

"Your file says you used to be a karate instructor before you joined up." Was that humility in his voice? Humble? Drill Sergeant Collier?

"Yes, Drill Sergeant," I answered, wondering what was coming next.

He smiled shyly and said, "You're going to have to teach me some of that." I could almost see the wheels turning in his head as he thought back to that day he challenged me at the firing range, and a few days later when he kicked the food tray from my hands.

"Oh sure, Drill Sergeant Collier," I said, knowing that it would never happen since there were only a few days left of training.

Besides, how could I teach karate to a dead guy?

People use all kinds of methods to vent their sense of helplessness and rage, including exercising, playing and watching sports, working excessively, overeating, abusing drugs, and watching pro wrestling. Psychologists would no doubt have mixed opinions as to how healthy it was for me to vent by "shooting" my drill sergeant. I do know that my rage diminished after that and my new attitude toward the man made it possible for me to get through the remaining days of boot camp virtually anxiety free.

Besides venting, there was another reason I shot the sergeant — revenge. He had embarrassed me and I needed to get even. Was fantasizing revenge a healthy thing to do? Again, psychologists would disagree and members of the clergy might even argue that a thought, especially one so intense, is the same as real action. I can't argue one way or the other about that, though I do know for sure that I couldn't have shot the drill sergeant for real.

I could shoot him in my mind, though, in that dark place where my warrior spirit needed to strike back.

CHOKE 'EM AND LEAVE 'EM

"This is car 740. Could I get a car to come by my location and help me out? I'm trying to arrest a driver here but his buddy is interfering."

"Roger that, 740," dispatch answered. "Car 732. Go to 82nd and Southeast Foster and give 740 a hand."

I told dispatch I was on my way. Portland Police car 740, my friend Dan, and I backed each other up every evening. First he would get a hot call and I would cover him and then I would get one and he would cover me. We both liked working alone and made a point of never asking for back up unless there was a serious need.

Dan had parked his car behind a ratty Ford sedan, the squad's overhead blues lighting the jewelry store parking lot like a disco. "What you got?" I asked, getting out of my car and flipping my collar up against the rain. There had been a steady downpour for several hours and a cold wind that whipped it in sheets. Dan held a cuffed man against the side of his police car, but his attention was on another man standing by the trunk of the Ford, a big man with glaring eyes.

"I stopped this guy for blowing through the red light and it turns out he's got a warrant. He's being agreeable, but his friend there is chipping his teeth and giving me a hard time. Just watch him so I can get my guy loaded and get out of here."

"No problem," I said, stepping between Dan and the man at the trunk. I nodded hello, but the big guy only glared back, his lips tight, neck cords tense, and his arms held rigid along his sides. He started to move around me, but I stepped into his path and told him to follow me as I moved out of the rain to a place under the eaves of the jewelry store. "What's going on tonight?" I asked, in a further attempt to distract him from what Dan was doing.

He looked at me for a second, and then over my shoulder at Dan closing the car door after placing his friend inside. Again he tried to step around me, but I blocked him a second time. "Why don't you let the officer do his job? If you interfere, you are going to jail with him."

For the first time he turned his complete attention toward me. "What?" he twisted his face, annoyed. "You threatening me?"

"No sir. Not at all," I said, looking into his eyes. "I'm making you a promise. You interfere and you're going to jail."

"Oh really? Tell me, officer," he sneered, looking me up and down. "Would you be so brave without your little badge and your big gun?"

"Yes. Yes I would," I said without breaking eye contact. A twitch had begun in the corner of his mouth. His eyes flashed.

Dan interrupted the moment. "I'd like to get going with my guy," he called out his window over the sound of the rain. He pointed at the Ford. "I'm just leaving his car here. You okay with that guy? I checked his name. No warrants. But don't let him drive the car. His license is suspended."

"Sure," I said with a wave. "Go ahead. We'll just chat for a moment 'till you're gone." The big guy stepped around me and headed toward Dan's car. I let him go this time since Dan's back door was locked and he was starting to pull away.

"I'll see you tomorrow, okay Eddie?" the guy said, tapping his finger on the back window. He cursed under his breath as Dan pulled out onto the street and accelerated away. He turned to face me. "I need to get something out of the Ford," he said. Then with an exaggerated bow, "With your permission, chief."

"Feel free," I said, gesturing toward the car. The sooner he got what he needed and left, the sooner I could go, too. I just wanted to make sure he didn't try to drive. When he opened the back door, I peered over his shoulder to see what he was leaning in to get.

"I just want to get a gas can out," he said, moving garbage around on the floor. "I got a car at home that's empty." When he straightened, he was holding a five-gallon gas can. "Like I was saying," he said turning toward me, "you cops think you are pretty tough."

The pounding rain increased in intensity. "Look," I said. "Your friend is gone; it's all over. He's going to get out in a few hours and the two of you can meet up again and do whatever it is that —"

He swung the gas can at me.

He cocked his arm way back and swung it at me the way John Wayne used to throw his big haymakers. It was a slow swing because the can was full.

I'm not sure what I did – I either blocked it somehow or leaned back and let it arc by my face — but a moment later I was behind him, with one of my hands holding his arm that held the can, and my other making like a nutcracker around his neck in the classic carotid artery restraint hold.

A few years later, one of our officers would kill a suspect with the hold. Due to the public outcry that followed, we were forbidden to use it except in deadly force situations. Constriction of the arteries on each side of the neck reduces the blood flow to the brain and, when executed perfectly, causes unconsciousness in about five seconds. The recipient usually regains a groggy consciousness in thirty seconds, though I've applied the hold on some people who have remained out for twenty minutes. The technique was an often-used favorite of mine, one that I taught in the academy.

The guy flapped his arms for two desperate seconds, and then, just as he tried to swing the can over his head to hit me again, he went suddenly limp, his weight heavy in the crook of my arm. I lowered him carefully onto the rain-puddled sidewalk and stepped back.

I looked at my watch: five minutes left before the end of my shift. I was soaked, tired and mad at this guy for putting me in a position to not only have to defend myself, but to force me to take him to jail and write reports, all of which would add up to an hour of wet, bone chilling overtime.

I looked around; there wasn't a soul on the street.

At my feet, rain splattered off the guy's sleeping face.

My watch now read three minutes before quitting time.

I thought about how warm and cozy my bed would be.

I made a decision. One that would get a lot of laughs over the years when I told the story to other cops, and one that would definitely get an officer fired today, probably arrested.

I got into my patrol car and drove away, leaving the unconscious man lying there, face up in the storm.

Thirty minutes later I was snug as a bug in my comfy, dry bed.

To this day, it's never been clear to me why I did that. I remember going through a period of being mentally and physically drained from all of man's inhumanity to man that I was experiencing daily on the job. I remember a sense of intense fatigue after I laid the guy down on the sidewalk, a sensation more mental than physical. I wanted to be lying on a tropical beach, but instead I was standing in the pouring rain, freezing, and having to defend myself from a guy who didn't know me, but thought it was okay to hit me in the head with a big gas can.

Sure, I could have taken him to jail. But in my tired mind, I didn't think he was important enough to bother with.

Did my actions show responsibility to my job as a police officer? No. Was it ethical of me to use my position as a police officer and as a martial artist to render a man unconscious and then not take care of him afterwards? No. Did he ever complain or did I ever hear from him again? No.

Did it feel really, really good to just leave him in the pounding rain?

Oh yes.

THE FAT GUY

I was sitting in my patrol car one day watching a crowded street corner in Portland's skid row when a fight erupted between two winos no more than twenty feet from my window. Before I could get out of my car, one man rammed an ice pick into the other man's temple. I grabbed the armed man, threw him to the sidewalk and scuffled with him briefly before I got him handcuffed. When my breathing and adrenaline had returned to normal, I felt a horrific pain in my shoulder and chest. I'd torn a pectoral muscle.

It was a debilitating injury, requiring an arm sling and weeks of agonizing physical therapy. I was given a desk job in the precinct, and I had to teach my karate classes from the sidelines instead of participating as I normally did.

During my duel careers in law enforcement and the martial arts, I was injured frequently, a reality I accepted as part of the violent territory in which I worked and played. Fortunately, most of my black eyes, jammed fingers and broken ribs, knees and toes never stopped me from training, at least in some fashion. I have always held the philosophy that if I injure my hand, I'll put more energy into my kicking drills, and If I break a toe, I'll work extra hard on hand techniques. The idea is to let the injury heal while getting stronger in another area of the martial arts.

The pectoral injury, however, was different than my others. Pain medicine kept me dopey all day and awake all night, though it didn't do a thing for the throbbing agony emanating from my shoulder. A week later, my other shoulder started to hurt. Whether it was from overuse, or just a psychological sympathy pain, it hurt badly enough that the doctor put that arm into a sling, too.

Working out was impossible; even leg stretching made my shoulders throb. I couldn't even drive my car because I couldn't raise my hands to grip the steering wheel. Feeling as weak and helpless as a child might have been a good lesson in humility, but I hated every minute of it.

A couple of weeks after the injury, I sat slumped in the passenger seat of a friend's car, grimacing at every bump while he drove me home from the grocery store. As we approached a stoplight, a beat-up car roared around our car and a blue car in front of us, and then cut abruptly back into our lane, nearly hitting the blue one. Inside the beat up car were three scruffy-looking people, two men and a woman. My cop instinct sensed a problem.

From the passenger side, a tall, fat, dirty man, leapt out, shouting and shaking his fists. At first it looked as if he were heading our way, but he stopped at the passenger's window of the blue car, shouting epithets at the elderly couple inside. He leaned his fat torso in the passenger's window, and jabbed his finger at the old man behind the wheel, who reached protectively for the white-haired woman and pulled her away from the guy.

I slipped out of my arm slings and started to open my door, but stopped when the guy extracted himself and took a couple of steps back toward the car he had gotten out of. Just as it looked like the road rage moment was over, he stopped and turned back toward the old woman, apparently having a second thought in his pea-sized brain. In the blink of an eye, he took a giant step toward the passenger's window and drove his ham-sized fist into the side of the old woman's face. She slumped forward into the dash.

I struggled laboriously to get out of the car as the fat guy ran around to the driver's side, shrieking for the old man to get out. Hoping to distract him, I shouted for him to stop. It worked. The guy spun, looked at me like a Grizzly looks at a picnic basket and began stomping toward me, screaming profanity and spraying froth.

"You have a problem, punk?" he screamed. The guy was my height but about forty pounds heavier. When I told him to leave the couple alone, he screamed even louder, flopping his arms up and down like a really mad barnyard chicken. "Who are you? Who are you telling me what to do? What are you going to do about it, punk?"

I told him I wasn't going to do anything about it, leaving out the fact that I couldn't move my arms. He sputtered, slobbered and snorted, which must have been the way he laughed, and then accused me of being a cowardly punk. I wanted a piece of him, just a small chunk out of his skull, but the pain in my shoulders, which felt as if railroad spikes had been driven into them, reminded me to play it cool. I gave him the "Christensen intimidation stare," but it didn't work. He returned with a hard stare of his own, one that said he wanted a piece of me too. Behind him, the blue car accelerated away, with the old woman still slumped against the dash.

As the fat guy and I stood glaring at one another, the driver of his car backed up until it was even with us. *Oh man, could this get any better?* Just as I wondered how I was going to deal with two more people, a woman called out from the back window for the guy to quit acting so stupid and get into the car.

The fat guy glared at me a moment longer, then slowly backed toward his car, looking me up and down with contempt and doing that snort thing again. He moved around to the passenger side and got in, shooting me one more glare over the roof of his car. He continued to stare through the window as his driver goosed the car through a red light.

I walked back to my car and plopped into the seat without saying a word to my friend. My hands, even my jaw trembled with anger and embarrassment. In spite of my adrenaline rush, my throbbing, dead shoulders made me feel impotent.

An hour after I'd returned home, my adrenaline still boiled. I was frustrated at feeling defenseless, something I hadn't felt since I was a child. Though the confrontation with the fat guy ended without anyone else getting hurt, I wasn't easily appeased. I replayed the scene in my mind, asking, "What would I have done if he had attacked the elderly man, or my friend, or me?"

My warrior spirit had to be vented and I had to restore my confidence. I went to the basement where I often trained by myself, though I couldn't move my arms to punch the bag and my injuries wouldn't tolerate the jarring from kicking it. There had to be a way I could have fought the guy had the situation accelerated. I always harped on my students to learn from their experiences, so it was time I practiced what I preached.

After some painful experimenting, which at first confirmed what I couldn't do, I found the answer: A finger in the eye. It doesn't take strength and it causes the biggest bully to have the worst day of his life. When heavyweight, boxing champion Muhammad Ali was asked during his heyday who he thought could beat him, he answered, "A little baby. With a just a poke of its finger in my eye."

I stood before the bag, superimposing the fat guy's face on the canvas. I found two little marks on the vinyl exterior and imagined them to be his eyes. I flicked my fingers at it, being careful not to make contact, which have sent the needle on my pain barometer into the red zone. I didn't extend my injured limb, but sort of launched my body at the bag, allowing my dead arm to go along for the ride while my fingers scraped across the bag's "eyes." The motion hurt a little, but I could live with it. I made the move again and again, each time my fingers flicking with increasing accuracy. I tried it with both arms, sometimes poking and raking with just one finger, other times with all five. When I found an angle that was virtually pain free, I moved as fast as I could.

Sometimes I would visualize the fat guy's hand reaching for me, and I'd move my body just enough to evade him and then twist in such a way to whip my fingers at the two marks. It must have looked strange, but it worked.

A half hour later I was drenched with sweat and my lungs ached for air. But it felt good because I was no longer helpless; my warrior spirit had surfaced, allowing me to find a solution to my problem. The feeling of satisfaction from that was greater than the fire in my shoulders.

Some people might argue that the solution to my sense of helplessness was a brutal one. For sure, jamming one's fingers into another's eyes does take a certain brutality. Could I do it if I met the fat guy again? If poking his eyes were the only way to defend myself or defend someone else, then yes, I would use it in a heartbeat. In fact, I would use it with extreme prejudice.

I thought a lot about what my basement workout accomplished that day. I reflected on how daily events often take away our feeling of being in control and how there are times when there isn't anything we can do about it. In reality.

In our minds, however, where the warrior spirit lives, we can use our imagination to reclaim at least a sense of control and power over our lives.

KAREN

Karen was in her early twenties and attractive. She studied karate with me for about eight months, adapting quickly to the tough martial arts regimen and passing the first two belt exams.

She stayed often after class to talk about her plans to further her education and to ask my advice on a few issues. Each time we talked, I sensed there was something else she wanted to tell me, something I could see stirring restlessly just below the surface and wanting to get out. I never pressured her, thinking it was best to let her choose the right time. Sure enough, one day she opened up.

Karen told me that she had had three violent experiences with men; on two of the occasions she had been raped. First, an uncle raped her when she was just twelve years old; the second one happened just a few months before she began studying karate, that time by her boss. A year earlier, her ex boyfriend had beaten her severely, breaking her nose.

None of the three attackers had been arrested. For some reason her family had decided not to report her childhood rape, and when her boyfriend assaulted her, she walked out on him instead of calling the police. The rape and assault by her boss were under investigation as we spoke, but she was thinking about dropping the charges. She said she wanted to forget it ever happened and just get on with her life.

Out of curiosity, I talked with the investigating detective the next day and learned that besides raping her, her boss had bitten her all over her body. It was an airtight case against the creep and all that was needed was for Karen to follow through with a complaint. I gave her this information the next night after class, but she was emphatic about dropping the charges. I suggested that I could arrange to have a female counselor from the rape victim's agency contact her, but she insisted that she just wanted to drop the whole thing and forget about it.

But I couldn't. As a police officer, I had investigated enough rape cases to know that most women suffer psychologically from their experience. Among other repercussions, they were often weighed down with a sense of helplessness and the ever present, nagging question of whether they could have done something differently.

Though Karen said she could deal with all the brutality she had experienced, it was apparent that she was struggling to hold in her emotions. I asked if she would be interested in trying an exercise I had found helpful in expelling pent-up anger and frustration, one that would allow her warrior spirit to surface and maybe give her some sense of empowerment. It might be a little frightening, I told her, because she would have to recreate mentally one of the violent situations that injured her. She would have to "see" it again and feel some or all of the same emotions she had when attacked. This time, though, there would be one big difference: She would get to apply her warrior spirit and defend herself with karate.

Karen was understandably reluctant, saying that she would like to think about it for a couple of days and let me know at our next class.

Over the next two days I began wondering if I had stepped out of line with her. Had I intruded on her personal business, her very intimate business? What if I had scared her off?

At the next class, however, there she was. She worked out with the other students without saying a word, but as soon as class was over, she walked up to me with a strong, purposeful walk, straightened the jacket of her uniform, jutted her jaw and said in a no-nonsense voice, "Let's do it."

We met the next day at the school and began the session with her detailing the assault by the ex-boyfriend. When I had all the information, I broke the assault into three phases and explained that we would examine each one as to how she could defend herself. She nodded, and with tight-lipped determination, shifted her body in a ready position.

The first thing the ex boyfriend did was to grab her hair, to which we worked out a defense. Once she understood the block, I stopped being her teacher and assumed the role of the attacker. When I reached toward her head, she easily blocked my hand aside. I repeated the move a tad quicker, and again she blocked it. For the next ten repetitions, I progressively increased my speed, and she successfully responded with faster and faster blocks.

She said that after he grabbed her hair, he jerked her toward him and punched her in the nose, which broke it and would leave it crooked for the rest of her life. She demonstrated how he threw the blow and we discussed the best block for it. When I threw the same punch, she blocked it perfectly. After a few repetitions, I began increasing the speed and she once again responded with faster and faster blocks. When I combined the two attacks, first grabbing at her hair and then throwing the punch, she blocked them both perfectly and effortlessly.

Now it was time for her to hit back. We worked out a response where she would block my attacks and then counter with a kick to the groin, a rake of the eyes and a punch to the throat. For the next fifteen minutes, I increased the speed each time I attacked. She looked frightened when I added verbal taunts, curses and called her the same names as the boyfriend had, but she stayed in there and blocked and countered as though her life depended on it.

By the end of the session, we were both drenched with sweat, and I was hurting where her uncontrolled blows had landed. Though she had a big scratch on her face from a missed grab, she looked more radiant and alive than I had ever seen her. I had to sit down, actually falling into the chair with exhaustion. But Karen charged toward the heavy bag as energetic as if she were just starting to work out, and for another ten minutes, assaulted it with more intensity than I had ever seen her exhibit.

Finished, she turned to me and smiled with at least fifty teeth. "I feel great," she laughed, punching the air with a fist. "This time I got the son-of-a-bitch good."

While this exercise ignited Karen's warrior spirit and replaced her feelings of helplessness and rage with a sense of control and perhaps not just a little revenge, I don't know how well it helped her in the long run. She continued to adamantly refuse help from a professional and a few months later relocated to another city.

It's strongly suggested that victims of sexual abuse inform the police and seek professional counseling.

CHAPTER FIVE

In the Presence of Warriors

I have had the wonderful opportunity to meet several martial arts masters during my years of martial arts study. Every one of them has been gracious, humble, knowledgeable, and all possessed incredible skill.

There is an almost tangible quality about martial arts masters that makes them stand apart from others. Some might call it a special aura, a presence or a dignified demeanor. By whatever name it's called, I believe it's a characteristic of those who have faced that warrior within and tamed it, or at least come to understand it.

It's been an honor to have learned from and been influenced by many great people I have met in the martial arts. It seems I have always met them at a time when I was complacent in my practice routines and smug that I knew all the answers. These true warriors showed up just in time to knock me down a peg or two and remind me that I still had lots to learn since learning in the martial arts never stops.

TONY

I met Tony at a friend's karate school in San Francisco where he was a guest instructor teaching chin-na, the Chinese art of twisting joints, tendons and muscles in painful directions. He was also a master of tai-chi chuan, a slow, rhythmic exercise and fighting art practiced by millions of people in his native country, China. When I met Tony, he was nearly fifty years old, though he looked thirty-five, and had thirty-seven years of martial arts under his belt.

He had been in the United States only two years, and because he was self-conscious of his English, he was quite shy about speaking in front of strangers. When he did, he didn't talk about himself but of his instructors and students back in China. He proudly showed two big scrapbooks jammed with pictures of them winning martial arts tournaments and even national titles.

Tony stood about five feet nine inches and weighed one hundred seventy pounds, much larger than the average Chinese. Besides his youthful appearance, he radiated an aura of dignity and power, and he looked majestic in his black kung-fu pants and white, crisply ironed Chinese top. There was a perfectly balanced grace to his walk, which was so soft and quiet that I wondered if he would leave footprints in snow.

A student accompanied Tony, a tall Caucasian man who seemed to be walking with great care and deliberation, as if in pain. The owner of the school, John, told me that the student was moving slowly because Tony had accidentally hurt him a couple of weeks earlier while demonstrating a technique during a seminar. The master had jerked his arm with such force that the six-foot three-inch man suffered an injury to his eyes, apparently as a result of whiplash to his head. The man had been taken to a hospital and was currently under a doctor's care.

I nodded that I understood, but in my mind I was having trouble believing that the Chinese instructor, or for that matter, any NFL linebacker, could have jerked the big man so forcefully. Seeing my disbelief and eager to show me the master's skill, John asked Tony if I could apply a few of my police restraint holds on him. Tony smiled and extended his arm.

My first technique was a standard wristlock, one that causes excruciating pain to the tendons of the wrist. It's a classic police hold used to control resisting subjects as well as applied to force them to walk from one point to another. After I had it in tightly, Tony asked quietly if the hold was on to my satisfaction. I answered, "Yes," but before I even finished uttering the "s," sound from the word, he was standing in front of me, arms folded, relaxed and smiling, as I stared in amazement at my hands, which were grasping nothing.

Much to the amusement of the other students in the room, Tony continued to escape effortlessly from every police control technique I applied; sometimes he nonchalantly tossed me to the mat as if the techniques were meaningless. The irony was that as a police officer I had successfully used these holds for years on some extremely violent people.

After I had exhausted my repertoire, Tony's student talked of his master's chi power. He said the Chinese believe that everyone has chi, a life force that circulates throughout our bodies. They also believe that after years of training in certain martial arts, tai chi for example, the practitioner can control his chi and channel it at will. I understood what he was saying because I had heard of masters who could move their chi to a specific part of their body to absorb impact from a blow, as well as channel it into their punches and kicks to create devastating force.

The student, knowing I was there to do a couple of magazine articles on other people, seized the opportunity to get publicity for his teacher by asking if I would like to test Tony's chi. Tony reacted with surprise at his student's question and appeared embarrassed and reluctant. John and the other students boisterously encouraged me, and even nudged me in Tony's direction. Clearly, I was being set up for something, but I couldn't refuse because my reputation and machismo were at stake. It's a guy thing.

After the student spoke with Tony for a moment, the master agreed to a small demonstration. The student told me to throw a punch at Tony, explaining that the master would deflect it with his forearm, but not counter attack. I agreed, thinking, How much harm can be done with a simple forearm deflection block? I would soon find out.

I launched a fairly fast punch at Tony's nose as he stood with his arms in a standard on-guard position, similar to a boxer's. When my punch neared his face, he moved his arm ever so slightly, brushing his forearm against mine. Though I barely felt his touch, I did feel an instantaneous jarring sensation slammed through my body, sending me backwards into John, who had been standing behind me in anticipation.

A strange swimming sensation filled my head and an overall weakness enveloped my body, making my legs wobble like those of a newborn colt. John supported me with his arm, looking at me with concern, although I noted a twinkle in his eyes and restrained laughter in his voice when he asked if I was okay. The others laughed uproariously.

When my head had cleared, John asked me to throw another punch at Tony, only harder. I didn't want to, but the others encouraged me. My ego has gotten me into a lot of trouble over teh years and this was going to be one more time. I nodded, and then punched hard and fast, holding nothing back. Again, Tony barely moved his forearm, brushing mine ever so slightly.

This time a bomb exploded in my brain as an invisible force slammed against my body. The room spun, sounds distorted and a hundred fizzle tablets bubbled in my skull. John and another set of hands held onto me as my feet struggled for stability as if on ice. The bubble storm in my head remained for several seconds and even after it began to clear, that strange weakness in my body remained.

My first coherent and organized thought was that there was no way I was going to punch at this guy again.

I have no definite explanation as to what happened that day. In recent years, the subject of chi, called ki in Japanese, has become controversial as more and more leading martial arts instructors discount its existence. Until Tony brushed my arm a couple of times, I was never sure what I thought of the stories I had read of chi masters who could inflict injury, illness and even death with a mere touch of their finger. Mostly I thought of them as just stories that may or may not contain an element of truth. What I experienced from this master, however, made me believe that chi, or some kind of awesome force definitely exists, and that there are people who have learned to tap into it.

Some scientists say that if there is such an entity as chi, it's simply adrenaline, a hormone we all have that increases physical strength when there is a threat to us. If that is all there is to it, how are some people able to control and harness it seemingly at will? Tony firmly believes that his power comes from chi. He said that many times when he trained and threw rapid combinations, his hands accidentally brushed against his own body causing him injury. He said he had developed his chi after many years of training, meditation, specific dietary restrictions and abstinence from sex.

Since my experience with Tony, I have continued to hear and read stories of chi power. Many of them are farfetched, but still fun to hear. While my experience may also seem farfetched, I know that it was real, amazing, and something I never want to feel again.

BRUCE LEE

In the spring of 1969, I attended a karate tournament in Washington D. C., one with champions from all around the country fighting to win the overall Grand Championship of all the competing black belts. Chuck Norris was there, so was Joe Lewis and lots of other familiar faces that had graced the covers of karate magazine for several years. The fighting was spectacular; the champions every bit as great as the magazines had said. I was beside myself with excitement, convinced my heart was going to thump right out of my chest. During an intermission, I walked to the back of the arena to stretch my legs and give my back a break from sitting on the bleachers. I had been in awe all day long, thinking that there wasn't anything that could top what I had seen at this tournament.

I had been standing there for only a couple of minutes when a sudden ruckus broke out behind me. I turned to see a group of about fifty people, some in karate uniforms, others in street clothes, stream into the arena from a small side door. Once inside, they pushed, crowded and stood on tiptoes in an effort to see someone in the center of their group. Curious, I moved toward them and joined in the struggle. At first, I couldn't see who ... and then I saw him. Oh man! Would this incredible day go on forever?

In the center of the crowd, sitting on the end of a table, was Bruce Lee.

In 1969, Lee was famous but he had not yet reached superstar status. He had been in the popular television series *Green Hornet* and had played a small role in another series called *Longstreet*. At the time of the tournament, he had just finished filming *Marlow*.

He sat in the back of the arena, perhaps to avoid the tournament crowd, though he seemed to enjoy those who had pushed in around him. If he was trying to be low key, his plan failed because word spread quickly and within five minutes he was surrounded by a horde. I maneuvered in closely to listen to what he had to say about filming *Marlow* and of his plans to go to Hong Kong to make another movie.

Later in the day, I watched him give sparring tips to a well-known tournament fighter named Louis Delgado. The soon-to-be idol of millions shuffled in and out of range with Delgado, throwing various hand blows and describing the benefits of each. Lee's speed was so over-the-top fast that it was at times difficult for my brain to accept it as real. There was magic in his movements, unlike anything I had ever seen even from top karate stars of the day. Watching him made me realize that I had thousands of miles to go in my study of the martial arts.

There was an aura around Bruce Lee, an odd light that made him stand out in the crowded room. Some have described him as cocky, but I didn't get that impression as I watched him interact with the crowd and work with Louis Delgado. For sure there was an attitude of confidence and a centeredness that conveyed that he knew who he was, what he was capable of and where he was going, but I saw it as an attitude of strength, positiveness, and an understanding of his warrior spirit. It was a quality that made him attractive in real life and a dynamic, and magnetic presence on the screen.

Bruce Lee went on to make several movies and become one of the biggest box office draws in history. He died suddenly in 1973 before he could see the incredible impact he was to make in the movies and on the martial arts world. Today, he still graces the occasional magazine cover and one or two books are published about him every year. I have been to his gravesite twice, once several years ago and again just recently. Incredibly, there is still a steady flow of visitors to it and to his son's, Brandon, who lies next to him.

There are martial artists today who are physically as good as Bruce Lee was, maybe there are some who are better, but so far, no one has equaled his charisma, innovativeness, genius and on-screen presence. Even if someone does come along with all these qualities, Bruce Lee will always remain our first martial arts hero.

Many people claim to have trained with Lee. I didn't. In fact, I was such a painfully shy brown belt, I didn't even have the nerve to say hello. But just seeing him that day, just being in the presence of true greatness, was a wonderful, energizing experience.

JOE LEWIS

It's virtually impossible to pick up a karate magazine and not see the name, Joe Lewis, or see a picture of his famous flying sidekick. This is as true today as it was thirty years ago.

In 1964, Lewis earned his black belt in Okinawa after only seven months of training. He entered his first point-karate tournament in the United States in the mid 1960s, the National Karate Championships, and after winning his division, went on to win the Grand Championship, the best of all the black belts. For the next six years, he won more than thirty major titles and was the only four-time national and three-time international champion. In 1970, Lewis became the United States Heavyweight Full-Contact Karate Champion and defended his title seven times. So fast, powerful and skilled was he that no opponent ever lasted longer with him than two rounds.

Joe Lewis has appeared on dozens of karate magazines covers, starred in several movies and appeared on many television talk shows. In 1999, he was the subject of a book titled *The Greatest Karate Fighter of All Time*, and countless articles have been written about his wins and his great fighting knowledge. Many top people in the world of karate consider Lewis a true modern-day master.

For the last several years, Lewis has traveled the world giving seminars on his insights into karate. It was at such a seminar that I had the opportunity to train with him.

Lewis is three years older than I. When he came to my city, I had just turned forty years old and was beginning to wonder what effect my age was going to have on my ability to practice and compete. I was eager to attend his seminar to learn from him, and also to see what Father Time (an often time cruel force) was doing to his skill.

I saw Lewis compete in 1969 at the same tournament where I saw Bruce Lee. His power was like an explosion, his timing impeccable, and like Lee, he had a presence about him that set him apart from other competitors. When he was in the ring, you watched only him; when he was on the crowded floor, your eyes naturally zeroed in on his every move.

Although I never talked to him at the tournament in1969, I felt a kind of kinship with him twenty years later at the seminar. We were both the oldest people in the room and we both had endured years of martial arts training. Although our paths had been different — he had become a sport and movie celebrity through his martial arts, whereas my interest was pragmatic because of my police work — karate was an integral part of both our lives.

I was amazed at how well Lewis had maintained his youthful physique. He had been a bodybuilder in his teens and at forty-three he still had a hard muscularity that emanated power. Though his face showed evidence of a few missed blocks during his years of full-contact fighting, there was still that California-boy handsomeness. Even the magnetic presence I had detected years earlier was there.

Lewis began his seminar with a lecture on his approach to training and fighting, information that was fresh and innovative. He presented concepts and principles that I hadn't even thought of and demonstrated various techniques that applied to them. His speed was extraordinary! Not only did his hands and feet move fast, he could move his entire body with such quickness that it was like watching a flickering old-time movie. He was here and in the blink of an eye, he was over there.

There were several advanced black belts in attendance, but not one of us could come close to matching his speed and unbelievable explosiveness. We could duplicate his movements — they were just basic hand and foot techniques – but ours, while black belt quality, paled in comparison.

For the first time in many years of studying the martial arts, I felt that my skill was inadequate. As I watched him move and punch and kick, I realized that if he decided to beat me up, there was not a darn thing I could do about it. I might have been able to launch an attack, but he would just be somewhere else before it landed.

I'm guessing that Lewis began his training with a certain amount of natural physical ability, but he reached his extraordinary level of skill as a result of training harder than other people. While training in Okinawa in his early years, he said that when most students stopped training for the day, he continued for another two hours. When everyone else trained three times a week, he trained seven times a week. He became a world champion because he was completely committed to the task. He didn't talk when he trained, he didn't play and he didn't waste time on frivolous techniques. He knew exactly what he wanted to do and where he wanted to go.

Training with Joe Lewis was an invaluable and humbling experience. His knowledge and skill went far beyond that place where most advanced karate students become complacent. He was the perfect example of a true expert who had reached a level of skill that most students of the fighting arts don't even know exists. Without argument, Joe Lewis is one of the greatest modern day martial arts masters of the last fifty years.

Someone once said that the definition of "master" (a term that is overused today) is a person who can teach it, describe it and do it expertly. Joe Lewis can do exactly that.

THE MAN IN THE WHEELCHAIR

I arrived at the tournament feeling good. It was one of those days that I just knew I was going to do well. I had trained hard for the competition and slept a solid eight hours the night before. So good and confident did I feel that I entered three kata divisions.

My first was the open black belt division. Fifteen other competitors had signed up to compete, some of the best the Northwest had to offer. Most of them were in their twenties, two were in their thirties and I was the old timer at forty. Everyone looked good: fast, powerful and full of fighting spirit. I came out on top, though, winning a large, first-place trophy.

The next event was the over-thirty-five-years-of-age division, usually a tough fight because most contestants are high-ranking black belts with many years of training. The older, more experienced competitors often bring a polish and maturity the younger ones lack. I won second place, which was fine with me because the winner, whose kata had a greater level of difficulty, definitely deserved first.

I still had lots of energy left after my second event and I was anxious to go again, especially since it was the black belt weapons' division, one in which I had won more first-place trophies than any other. There were lots of competitors, but I managed to tie for first place, and after repeating our performances, I edged out the other guy to capture the first place trophy. I happily lined up of with the competitors to await the judges' presentation of the awards. It's always fun to win, so I was having a good time. I felt good, I had competed well and I had been getting lots of pats on the back all day. As the saying goes: "It was all about me."

And then I saw the guy in the wheelchair.

I had noticed him from across the gym before my first event, but because my concentration was on the competition, I paid him little attention. This time though, since his chair was parked in front of the bleacher, just a few feet from where I had finished competing, I saw him in greater detail.

He was only in his twenties but his body had been twisted and knotted by a cruel stroke of nature. His lifeless, pencil-thin legs were partially covered by a weathered, plaid blanket, and his hands, claws really, gestured erratically. His eyes, which revealed an intense intelligence, were looking directly at me, though his head twisted and turned, and his mouth opened and closed almost rhythmically.

Even when the head judge called for the competitors to step up for the presentation of the trophies, I couldn't take my eyes away from him. The third-place winner was announced first and then the second place winner. When the judge called my name for first, I waved at the crowd, then my eyes fell again on the man in the wheelchair. He was twisting about frantically and clapping with large, wild swings of his arms. His eyes reflected the excitement he felt, though any sound he made was drowned out by the applause from the crowd.

All the pride and satisfaction I'd been feeling since the tournament began dissipated into the air. I suddenly felt undeserving and holding my trophy felt uncomfortable. Not wanting the man in the wheelchair to see me with it, I handed it to a student to hold, and then I walked quickly to the far side of the gymnasium and sat on the floor.

The man in the chair was now absorbed in a sparring match, clearly thrilled with what he was seeing. He cheered and applauded the competitors, his entire crooked body alive with excitement about what he was witnessing, and what he would never be able to do.

I have always been thankful for being healthy and able to practice and teach karate, an endeavor that is so physically demanding. I know I have been blessed to have spent so many years doing what I love to do. Watching the man in the wheelchair made me feel these things even more intensely. Watching him twist, writhe and contort himself in his chair, I thought of the expression, "There but for the grace of God go I." Due to nature's selection process, he had been made a prisoner of his own body, while I was given one that was strong and healthy.

Just as I started to feel sorry for him, it struck me how happy he appeared. He had several friends with him and he was enjoying the tournament. He may not have been a contestant, but he was participating by applauding and cheering the competitors from his place in his chair.

The more I watched him, the more I realized that he was more of a fighter than all of us who wore karate uniforms with colored belts wrapped around our waists. He didn't just compete one weekend a month in a two-minute round of pretend fighting. He had to fight every day, not a pretend one, but a real battle against a formidable opponent that never went away. My efforts paled in comparison.

Clearly, the man in the wheelchair was the real warrior.

CHAPTER SIX
Fear

I've experienced the copper-taste of fear on many occasions.

I can still feel how my stomach churned as my Vietman-bound airplane, full of fresh soldiers, descended through the dark sky toward a small airport in Bien Hoa. How my heart slammed against my chest when the cabin lights went suddenly dark, followed by the captain's worried voice over the intercom telling us they would remain off so as not to draw enemy fire from the ground. I remember pressing my young face against the glass and peering wide-eyed at the brilliant artillery flashes below, and feeling so full of dread, confusion, excitement and numbing fear.

As a police officer, I've heard the *ziiiing* of passing bullets, felt knawing anxiety over what was waiting for me on the other side of a door, and felt my breathing stop when I saw a hand reach for a gun. As a karate fighter, I've felt my flesh-and-blood legs turn to stone when looking into the eyes of a competitor who was totally focused on hurting and embarrassing me.

What follows in this section are three situations in which I've felt fear all the way to my bone marrow. In one, it controlled me, in another I managed to do my job, and in the third situation, I had to struggle to function in its aftermath.

I have no scientific data to support this, but I believe that our biorhythms (an inner rhythm that seems to control biological processes) have much to do with the level of fear we experience in a given situation. As a soldier in Vietnam, street cop in Portland, and a martial artist since 1965, I have always accepted fear to be part of my experiences. What has always fascinated me, however, is the intensity of it, sometimes minimal, sometimes over-the-top.

When I was a police officer, there were times when I responded to calls that were, in police parlance "no big deals," yet for some reason I would be fearful, complete with nervous sweat and the jitters. Other times, I would drive calmly and anxiety free to "hot calls" where there was an expectancy of danger, such as a "man with a gun" or a gang fight. During my twenty-nine years in law enforcement, I responded to thousands of calls for help, the no-big-deal ones and the hot ones, enough of each to know which ones elicited specific responses in me. That is why I found it perplexing whenever I responded abnormally.

The fight-freeze-flight response given to us by Mother Nature is responsible for humankind surviving into the new millennium. But police officers don't have the luxury of allowing these natural responses to control their actions. They can fight, but under the strict mandate of agency policy and law, which is to control the threat with minimum force. Fighting with control, however, can be difficult when the battle is a desperate one not to get killed. Flight is not an option for law enforcement because officers are paid to go *to* the trouble, often while citizens are running from it (as seen in the story "The Shooting"), which follows. Freezing is not an option for officers, unless the threat is a giant grizzly bear and lying motionless is the best option.

I have known officers who are comfortable enough with themselves to admit being so fearful at an incident that they couldn't function. One aggressive officer, who worked a busy, gang-infested district, told me that on one occasion he was at home getting ready to go to work when he froze. He was slipping on his shoes, he said, when suddenly, without warning, he couldn't move, not one muscle.

104

A minute or two passed before he had the strength to call out to his wife to come help him lie down. After several minutes of deep breathing, he still couldn't get up to and finish dressing, and after thirty more minutes, he knew he couldn't go to work. He called in and said he had the flu.

The next night he went to work without a hitch and has never had a repeat episode.

THE CALL

I was parked on a side street writing a report when dispatch gave the neighboring beat car a call in my district. "See the bartender at the Keg 'n More Tavern. Report of a very large, violent drunk assaulting patrons and tearing up the place."

I reached for the mike to tell dispatch that I would take the call since I had finished my reports and I was only a few blocks away. I wrapped my fingers around the mike and began to pull it from its holder. But I couldn't: without warning, my hand, my entire arm, froze. No matter how I willed my hand to extract the mike from its slot, my muscles refused to respond.

At this point in my career, I'd responded to at least two-dozen tavern brawls, always going without hesitation. But this time a weird, powerful feeling washed over me, and to this day I can't describe the sensation other than to say that it compelled me not to go to that tavern. I just sat there dumbly, my heart thumping madly and sweating as if I'd just sprinted a mile.

Again I tried to pull the mike away from the holder, and again my arm failed me. I listened as dispatch got another car to back up the assigned one, praying the officers wouldn't drive down the street and catch me sitting there. What would I say? What would they think of me? I'd be ruined in the department. Still, my hand couldn't retrieve the mike.

I sat there like a bump on a log for about ten minutes, listening as the cars announced their arrival at the tavern and suffering with guilt during the dead air that followed. I wondered if I would be able to respond if one of them came on shouting breathlessly for more back up. About three minutes later, although it felt like thirty, one of the officers notified dispatch that they had the suspect in custody and would be taking him to jail.

During my career as a city cop, I found myself in the middle of riots, gang fights, bar brawls, shootings, knifings, countless resist arrest situations and a host of other violent encounters. Why I froze that time, and only that time out of twenty-nine years of police work, I haven't a clue.

I do know that I couldn't look at myself in the mirror for a long time after.

THE SHOOTING

Tom and I had been on duty for a couple of hours and, though it was only 10 a.m., Portland's streets were blistering under an ugly August sun. It was going to be a killer of a day.

While waiting for Tom, who was inside a corner grocery buying cigarettes, I slumped in the seat behind the steering wheel, exchanging waves with the street regulars and listening to some mellow jazz coming from the car radio. Just as I was losing the battle to keep my eyelids open in the oppressive heat, dispatch called our number.

"832?" Not her usual bored tone.

"832 here," I answered, looking toward the store for Tom.

"832, you've got a man carrying a rifle into the Malcom Building, 222 N.W. Abraham. He's described as a white male, 180 pounds, approximately fifty-five years old and wearing a tan jacket."

106

I rogered the call and shouted out the window at my partner, who was now standing in the store's doorway talking to the clerk. Dispatch called us again as Tom slid in. "Car 832 and all covering cars, our caller says the subject got off on the fifteenth floor. Another caller says the man is armed with a shotgun."

"We're on our way," I said, handing the mike to Tom. I flipped on the blue lights and sliced our car into traffic. A half block later, a back up car rounded a corner and inched up to our rear bumper, its overhead lights also pulsating.

Tom and I rode silently, contemplating the possibilities. The armed man could be just a businessman bringing his hunting weapon to work so that on his lunch break he could take it to a local gun shop for repairs. We had had similar calls before and, though it was a stupid thing to do, it wasn't illegal. We would just chew out the citizen for scaring everyone – especially the police. This was probably the same situation.

I was wrong.

"832 and all covering cars..." her voice was higher pitched now and her attempt to control her delivery pace obvious. *"... we have several reports of shots being fired on the fifteenth floor now."*

I flipped on the siren and Tom jabbed a fresh cigarette between his lips. The patrol car's siren behind us chorused with ours, along with that of a third police car's that rounded the corner in front of us.

"All cars responding to the Malcom Building...more shots have been fired, one person reported down."

My heart couldn't have pounded harder if I were running to the call; Tom sucked hungrily at his cigarette. Again we silently considered the possibilities. Was there only one, armed person? If there were others, were they shooting at each other? If it was a lone gunman, was he shooting people at random? Were we going into a hostage situation? Would we have to shoot the guy?

I slid to a stop in front of Malcom Building, along with three other patrol cars and an ambulance. Dozens of people poured out

107

the glass doors onto the sidewalk, some of them shouting hysterically about a gunman, others weeping, all terrified.

We pushed our way through the crowd to the glass doors and then struggled against more people to reach the bank of elevators. Two EMTs, a female officer named Trish, and Tom and I, pushed our way into one, while other officers positioned themselves in the lobby so they could watch the door to the stairs and the bank of elevators in the event the gunman tried to exit. The doors to ours swished shut and we began ascending to the fifteenth floor.

Dispatch crackled through our portables that the suspect still had the shotgun and was wandering somewhere on the floor. We made a quick plan how we were going to exit the elevator. Tom and I would go left and Trish would go right; the EMTs would remain pressed against the back wall until we had the situation under control. We unholstered our weapons.

The elevator doors slid open to utter bedlam: people shouting, screaming, all running to our right. We looked out for a long moment. Was the suspect in the crowd? If he hid the shotgun behind him, we wouldn't know who he was right away, though he would definitely know who we were. We exited the elevator as we had planned.

"Thank God…you're here," a man in an expensive gray suit wheezed, grabbing Tom's arm. He jabbed his finger toward a pair of closed double doors at the end of the hall, the direction from which people were running. He spoke in gasps: "He's…in there…the doctor's office…he's killed…Doctor James… shotgun"

A moment later, the hall had changed from chaos to eerie silence. Completely exposed, Tom, Trish and I slid along the walls toward the double doors, our guns at the ready. My watering eyes bore into the doors, expecting any moment for them to burst open, followed by the mad gunman spraying fire and lead into our bodies.

We stopped our advance about ten feet from the doors and stood motionless, watching, waiting. Our breathing was the only sound in the room, but in our respective ears, it was our thumping hearts.

I was aware of a sense of readiness in my mind —a readiness to kill. From the moment I got out of the car, I had been busy pushing through the crowd, riding the elevator, listening to updates on the radio and planning our exit into the hall. But now, in this dead time, I had a moment to think about what might happen in the next few minutes, or seconds. Though I didn't want to shoot anyone, I was acutely aware that I would if the gunman came out those doors with his weapon at the ready. I would shoot him without hesitation.

Trish and Tom stationed themselves on each side of the door; I flattened myself along the wall next to Trish. Then we waited. And waited. After a few minutes of nerve-wracking silence, we exchanged glances, each of us thinking the same thing: We had to go in.

Behind me — the sound of a door latch. I spun, crouched and thrust my gun, ready to fire. Five feet away, a white-haired, elderly lady peered through a partially open door, her eyes widening at the sight of the business end of my gun.

"Shut the door," I hissed. It closed quickly. I turned back.

Tom and Trish had alerted on something. I followed their eyes to a turning doorknob on the double door closest to Trish. We pressed ourselves against the wall, our guns at the ready. The door cracked an inch for a moment and then opened all the way inward, exposing Trish's position. Her eyes widened; her hand white-knuckled the grips of her gun. Tom and I couldn't see what she was seeing.

"Drop the shotgun," she barked. "Drop it now!"

Tom and I stepped away from the wall and took positions on each side of Trish, pointing our weapons at...a blood-splattered man standing no more than six feet away, holding a shotgun, its barrel pointing at our feet. His face was clearly insane: eyes glazed over, a large, toothy smile on a blood-polka-dotted face. I tightened my index finger on the trigger, aiming at the bridge of his nose.

We could have fired, but we didn't. Perhaps we would have on another day, but on this one, we all thought in concert. The man's eyes looked at us, though it was obvious he was focusing far away on another place that only he could see. He might have been able to fire before we could have reacted, but instead, he allowed the shotgun to slip slowly from his fingers and drop to the floor.

I jammed my gun into my holster, lunged forward and slammed my palm against his shoulder, knocking him off balance before I kicked his feet out from under him. He landed with a pronounced thud, and I grabbed his arm to force him over onto his stomach. Tom picked up the shotgun and handed it off to someone in the hall. The suspect struggled and screamed over and over that he was the supreme judge, jury and executioner of the universe.

While I snapped on the handcuffs, Tom, the EMTs and a couple of other police officers rushed into a back office. I looked up afterwards and noticed, for the first time, a middle-aged woman, apparently a secretary, leaning against a desk, weeping loudly. Her dress, arms, legs and face were covered with blood and small red chunks of...brain matter.

Then Trish came into my focus, kneeling beside me (had she been there the whole time?), her face an expression of shock. "I almost shot him," she said, her voice monotone and just above a whisper. "My finger was squeezing the trigger...and, and ... I was about to shoot him." Then louder, "I was going to kill him if he didn't drop the shotgun! I was squeezing the trigger –"

I slapped her upper arm hard. "Trish!" She blinked and looked at me, her face confused. "I need your help here," I said softly

She looked down at the gunman. "What..."

"Help me search his jacket, Trish."

She shook her head as if clearing fog. "Okay," she said with a little more life, and then began going through his pockets. We found fifteen shotgun shells in his pants, shirt and jacket pockets.

I looked up to see Tom walk out of the back office, his face ashen. "You don't want to go back there," he said numbly. "The doctor's head...it's gone."

We lifted the suspect to his feet and walked him through the madhouse that had erupted in the hall: people crying and holding each other, police radios blaring and TV crews with glaring lights jockeying for position. As we worked our way through the crowd to the elevator, the gunman laughed hysterically and shouted repeatedly that he was the supreme executioner. Even after we got him inside, he continued his mad diatribe throughout the descent. In the building's basement, Tom, Trish and I placed him into the backseat of a waiting police car, and then watched silently as it sped away, en route to jail.

That night the story was all over the television and the front page of the newspaper. We learned that he had been a patient of the psychiatrist, but we never learned why he walked into the doctor's office and killed the man who was trying to help him. According to the secretary, she had been sitting at the desk taking dictation from the doctor when the gunman burst through the door and, without a word, fired the shotgun five times into the doctor's face, reloaded and fired three more times into his chest.

A few weeks later, the courts decided the man was too mentally ill to stand trial, and he was sent to a mental institution.

After leaving the shooting scene, Tom, Trish and I drove to the precinct. We were emotionally and physically drained, but we had to write reports and then go back out on the street to work until 4:00 p.m. Tom and I handled other calls that day, but I have no memory of what they were.

Each of us dealt with the experience in our own way. I wanted to go with Tom and Trish after work to knock back a few drinks, but I had to teach karate that evening. In lieu of alcohol, I pushed myself in class until I could barely move and then went home and slept fitfully. I kept seeing the gunman's blood-splattered face and feeling my finger squeeze the trigger. Sometimes, I dreamt that the man raised the shotgun toward me. I'd see fire leap from his barrel, and feel jagged pellets rip into my body.

I had trouble going into high-rise buildings for a long time afterwards. I would break out in a cold sweat in elevators and then have to force myself to get off and step into the hall. Simply opening office doors would send my heart thumping out of my chest.

There are some police officers, military people and martial artists who feel that warriors should be able to suck it up and deal with such events without being traumatized afterwards. When I was younger, I was one of them, but as I have gotten older, and I hope wiser, I realize that sane people will experience fear and emotional repercussions from horrific incidents, no matter how well-trained and prepared they are. Training increases the warrior's chance for success, but it doesn't eliminate emotion, though it may reduce its intensity.

Experiencing fear and emotional trauma is a natural result of facing life-threatening circumstances. There is no shame in it, and it certainly doesn't mean the person is less of a warrior because he feels these emotions.

What should be of concern is the person who doesn't feel anything.

OFFICER DOWN

The bullet ripped through my partner's chin, through his tongue and lodged next to his top vertebrae.

Five minutes earlier, we had received a call on an armed robbery at a liquor store with the suspect last seen running toward a nearby park. My rookie partner, John, was behind the wheel, first accelerating us through the parking lot of the hilly, tree-thick city park, and then rounding a corner onto a short street that connected to a city street.

"There's Anderson," I said, pointing toward an officer crouched by a six-foot-high wooden fence that separated the street from a backyard. Anderson was holding his gun in one hand and gesturing toward the fence with his other.

"He went over the fence," he whispered urgently as John and I scrambled from the car, pulling our weapons. "If you two have this part of it, I'll go around the far end to block him from coming out that way."

John moved toward the fence. "I'll check the yard," he said, and began scooting himself up. I sprinted through tall grass toward the other end of the fence in case the suspect chose that way to leave the yard. Unless the man ran across the yard away from us, we had him boxed in.

At my end of the fence, I found a huge, overgrown walnut tree, its heavy branches draping all the way to the ground. Just as I began to push through them, I heard a bang from the direction of our car. Part of the fence must have fallen, I thought. No, it was a shot. But it didn't sound like a shot, or did it? Maybe John shot at the suspect. No, that wasn't a shot; it wasn't loud enough. With one hand on my holstered gun, I pushed deeper into the branches to get to the other side of the fence to see what was going on.

I pushed aside a particularly heavy one and looked into a perspiring face and a set of crazed eyes, no more than a foot away. A frightened homeowner? No, he had the beard, heavy build and wore the purple T-shirt described by dispatch. And he held a gun at his side.

He lifted the weapon in slow motion until I could see into the blackness of the yawning barrel. Ever so slowly, his thumb moved onto the hammer and clicked it back into the cocked position.

In one fluid motion, I snapped the big branch into his face and dived to the ground behind a Volkswagon Bug. I crawled along its side and then scooted up on my knees next to the front fender. I quick-peeked a couple of times over the sloped hood, hoping the suspect wasn't on the other side doing the same thing. He wasn't. He was about fifty yards away, standing by a car that the homeowner had parked in his yard while he washed it. Fortunately, that man had gone into the house to get something, because now a desperate gunman stood next to his car, raising his gun in my direction. I fired mine first.

The man spun and fell face down onto the ground. I waited for a moment, watching to ensure that he didn't get up. Not seeing movement, I walked slowly toward him, my gun extended. "Where are you hit?" I asked, standing next to his prone body, my barrel at the back of his head.

"You missed," he groaned. We learned later that my round had smacked into the upraised car trunk and that the sound of the impact fooled the suspect into thinking he had been shot. Once he realized he hadn't been, it was too late because he saw me advancing and pointing my gun at his head. It would have been hard for him to run off anyway, as he had broken his ankle when he jumped over the fence moments earlier. I spotted his gun laying in the grass a few feet away, its hammer still back.

As I applied the handcuffs, I heard a feint voice call my name from across the yard.

From where I knelt by the suspect, I could just barely see John's head and shoulders above the other side of the fence, holding his chin with one hand, blood covering both. He waved weakly with his other hand and then dropped out of sight behind the fence. A moment later, a siren wailed from the same place I had just seen him.

Neighbors, who had seen everything through their front windows, later told us what they witnessed. They saw me run toward the end of the fence and John scoot over it, both of us clearly unaware that the suspect was just on the other side, leaning against the fence and pointing his gun upward. As John's head came over the top, the suspect fired, the round striking him in the chin. The neighbors saw John fall off the fence and into the tall grass, struggle to his feet, only to fall back down again.

Growing weaker by the second, John worked his way to his feet again, looked over the fence, called out my name and waved. He was unable to say more because blood was pumping down his throat. He fell again, tried to get up, but couldn't. He crawled over to the police car and somehow gathered enough strength to crawl in and retrieve the mike. Still unable to speak, he desperately tripped the siren switch before falling unconscious and tumbling out of the car.

As dozens of police cars screamed to the area, I waited with the downed suspect until back-up officers found me and helped take the gunman into custody.

John's heart stopped for forty-five seconds, but with help from an ambulance crew, it beat again. At the hospital, where John spent several weeks, the doctors decided to leave the bullet next to his vertebrae, determining that it was too risky to remove. Months later, he tried to come back to work, but the pain in his neck was too great. He was eventually placed on disability and never returned.

The gunman received a 40-year sentence, but he was released on good behavior after serving only two and a half years.

That was the first of three shootings I would be personally involved in as a police officer. When this first one happened, the police department didn't know how to deal with officers involved in traumatic incidents, so I was sent back on patrol a day later, though I was intensely apprehensive and still shaken from the experience; I was literally in an emotional fog.

Today, most police psychologists advise wisely that officers who have been involved in a deadly force situation not return to work until they are convinced in their minds that they could shoot again. No officer wants to take a life, but he should know in his mind that he is capable of doing it. If on the other hand, he knows he can't, he should not be on the street where his function is to protect people.

I know one SWAT officer who took a month off after he was forced to kill a suspect who first stabbed a pregnant woman and then tried to stab him. When the officer returned to work and changed into his uniform, he knew instantly that he couldn't shoot again if a situation required it. So he took more time off, returning only when he felt psychologically ready. A week later, he was forced to kill again, this time a bank robber who had taken a teller hostage and was holding a gun against her head.

When I returned to work, my first call was an armed robbery alarm, a call considered by officers to be either false, or high-risk if real. All the while I was racing to the scene, I wondered if I was ready to use deadly force. Fortunately, I never had to find out because the alarm was a false one, but I trembled for many hours afterward thinking what might have been.

For several days after John had been shot, I felt drained, as if someone had pulled a plug somewhere and my life force had emptied out. I spoke no more than I had to and when I did, I could barely talk above a whisper.

Had my partner's near-death experience, and my looking down the same barrel that had shot him, destroyed my warrior spirit? I thought so for a while, but then I learned about a thing called "adrenaline dump" a phenomenon that occurs after a traumatic experience. My exhaustion was not from a loss of my warrior spirit, but from having come down from my drug-like high, those intense minutes when my adrenaline had flooded through my body in fight-to-survive mode.

I also learned from a martial arts teacher that one aspect of being a warrior is to continue in the face of adversity, to "do what needs to be done," as he put it. Thinking back on the days after that first shooting, I'm proud to say that I did just that. I returned to work, put on my uniform and went out on the street to answer my hot calls and back up other officers on theirs.

Sometimes the strongest people are those who don't give up. I didn't want to come back to work, but I returned and did what had to be done.

CHAPTER SEVEN

Lessons Along the Way

Most of us learn quickly that there are some things in life we just have to accept because fighting them; whining about them and wishing that they didn't exist won't make them go away. I've learned that being a warrior is to recognize those things and then figure out how to work through them, around them and with them. Here are some examples.

RUDE PEOPLE

I don't like rude people. I don't like it when they crowd in front of me in lines, I don't like to be cut off on the freeway and I hate it when someone bumps against me on a crowded sidewalk and then keeps right on going as if I were not worthy of a simple "excuse me."

There was a time in my life when I would strike back at rude people. When someone crowded in line, I would boldly step up and challenge him with my attitude and hard stare, and I would be more than ready to do battle should they challenge me back.

I obey the speed limit. If it's posted 60 MPH, I do 60, usually to the aggravation of motorists behind me who want to go 65 or

70. Some of them feel it's necessary to "punish" me for my slow driving by tailgating, honking, swerving around my car and coming within an inch of hitting it as they cut back into my lane.

This used to enrage me and set me on a course of road rage. I would test tailgater's reflexes by stomping my brake pedal and smiling into the rearview mirror as they skidded and swerved to avoid my rear bumper. On single-lane highways, I'd turn on my left turn signal just as a fast driver was beginning to pass on my left, and get a big laugh out of watching him try to control his skid. I'm ashamed to admit that many times I did these stupid antics when my family was in the car, which not only endangered my life and the lives of the occupants of the other car, but also of those closest to me.

Then I met Sifu. Sifu, which is Chinese for teacher, is a tenth-degree black belt living and teaching his fighting art in San Francisco. Over the years, I have trained with him in karate, jujitsu and in the stick fighting art of arnis. He also taught me how to teach, how to run a school and, most importantly, how to get along with people.

Driving conditions in San Francisco during rush hour are a prime example of insane, raw aggression. It's every driver for him or herself, where only the strong and courageous get to change lanes, and the meek miss their exits. One time, Sifu was driving his old van and I was sitting in the passenger side wondering if I would survive this traffic riot to fly back home the next day.

Sifu drove as if he were sparring an opponent: He faked, bobbed, weaved and attacked. Instead of letting out with a karate yell, he tapped the horn and giggled as if the metal madness was all fun and games. He was fast and aggressive, but through it all, he maintained a calm demeanor, the same demeanor he displayed in his school. I never once saw him resist or retaliate another driver, no matter what they did to him.

Right after Sifu had braked especially hard to avoid crashing into a pickup that had swept across three lanes without signaling,

I asked if he ever wanted to pull one of these crazy drivers out and beat him into a weeping pile.

"What?" He looked over at me as if the idea had never occurred to him. "No," he answered simply.

"But why not," I persisted. "If I had to drive in this every day, I would leave a trail of dead bodies in my wake. I wouldn't tolerate people treating me like this."

He changed lanes quickly to avoid hitting yet another car that had cut in front of us, and then said, "Well, I just don't let what these people do be that important to me. If I did, I would always be upset, feel badly and maybe even try to hurt someone. You know, there will always be rude people, people who weave in and out of our lives every day, just like these cars weave in and out of the lanes. But I choose not to let what they do be that important since they're only in my life for a few minutes. Sometimes not even that long."

Sifu's simple philosophy hit me like a jab in the nose, a flash of enlightenment. I had been letting rude people, people I didn't know or would probably never see again, control how I felt. Most of them had been, as Sifu said, in my life for only a few moments, but I had allowed their conduct to be so important to me that it influenced my behavior and how I felt for hours afterwards. Pretty dumb.

On the flight home the next day, I continued thinking about what my teacher had said. I wondered if I could possible live his simple philosophy.

Later, as I made my way down the concourse, a man, probably hurrying to catch a flight or greet a loved one, slammed into my shoulder as he ran past me. I had to do a quick shuffle to keep from falling, but my hand-held luggage went flying.

I turned quickly and saw that he continued to run without so much as a glance back to see if I was okay. Instantly, my face flushed with anger and adrenaline roared into my muscles. Just as I started to yell at him, I heard Sifu's words: *You know, there will always be rude people, people who weave in and out of our lives every day, just like these cars weave in and out of the lanes. But I choose not to let what they do be that important since they're only in my life for a few minutes. Sometimes not even that long."*

I hesitated for a moment, torn between the meaning of Sifu's words and my desire to go after the guy. After a moment of indecision, it occurred to me that the man was already gone, lost somewhere in the crowd. Out of my life.

I began walking along the concourse again, not in the direction the man had run, but in my original direction. Already my anger was dissipating, and I could feel a slow smile spreading across my face.

ON GETTING OLDER

I began training in karate at the age of nineteen. Although I had a previous back injury that I eventually overcame with help from the karate exercises, I was strong and full of energy. I believed I had no limitations and I never let doubt get in my way.

We didn't have the safety equipment that protects everything from our feet to our head that we have today, so I received a lot of injuries in those early years. I always had bruises, sprains and the occasional broken bones, but because I was young and healed quickly, I didn't give them much thought.

In my twenties I could do everything in karate. I believed that pain was part of the martial arts, a bump on the path to self-knowledge. It didn't matter that my jumps, somersaults and assorted flips, rolls and dives were executed painfully on hardwood and cement floors because I was enjoying the appreciative "oohs" and "ahhs" from people watching. Nor did I care that the techniques were far from the reality of real fighting.

I had workouts that were of biblical proportions, though I didn't think of them that way at the time since my energy knew no bounds. Without giving it a second thought, I'd work out for entire afternoons — sparring, forms, punching and kicking drills, heavy bag work and skipping rope. Once a week, I'd throw kicks for a quarter mile around a high school track, and then stagger on depleted legs back to my car. My training partner and I sparred full contact without protective hand and foot gear. We were at least smart enough to keep face contact moderate, but we went all out slamming hard kicks and punches into each other's body. The more it hurt, the more we liked it.

I reached my full potential in my thirties, peaking around thirty-five. I had good flexibility, strength, speed and aggressiveness, and I still enjoyed training hard and pushing myself as far as I could go. I met many top people in the fighting arts, won lots of accolades and awards, and I like to think that I gave a lot back, too. The martial arts were a huge part of my life then and I was completely happy and content with what I was doing.

Toward the end of my thirties and into my early forties, I began thinking about my advancing age. Physically, I wasn't feeling any limitations, but the time was approaching when I would. I felt it was important not to grow stale in my training and to have a clear direction as to what I wanted to accomplish in the martial arts.

My first goal was to compete in tournaments and to do well; I wanted my personal record to show wins in my twenties, thirties and forties. My second goal was to earn a black belt in a third fighting art, jujitsu. Establishing those two goals would provide direction in my workouts and the drive to make training fun and productive.

The first half of my forties was amazing. I won over fifty trophies in competition and earned the black belt in jujitsu, and a second one three years later. Just as I was starting to believe that I was on an unstoppable roll, I injured my shoulder severely in a street brawl in my duties as a police officer. It happened the day before I was to defend my title at an annual tournament and, though

I didn't know it at the time, the injury was so severe that I would never again be able to tolerate the rigors of training for competition.

As if to remind me that I was no longer the same guy I was in my twenties and thirties, recuperating from the shoulder injury was a long process that seemed to ignite other old injuries. Most of the time I accepted my advancing age, but other times it sent me into a gray funk.

One morning I woke up and, seemingly out of nowhere, decided that I was not going to allow age to have its way with me. I knew I couldn't stop its sadistic, forward advance, but there were things I could do to slow down the usual accompaniments of aging: physical weakness, extended belly and shortness of breath. If I wanted to enjoy the martial arts, I had to get back into top condition and get my shoulder working again.

I began paying close attention to eating properly, I hit the weights harder, including my shoulder therapy exercises, and I made sure I was getting plenty of aerobic work. That took care of the body, but I also needed to nurture the psyche. Just as I did at the end of my thirties, I established goals to avoid falling into that easy rut of maintaining the status quo. I grouped them into three sections: a short-term goal that I could reach in two to three weeks, a middle-term one that would take two to six months, and a long-term goal to reach in one or two years.

That did the trick. The shoulder eventually healed, but by then competition was no longer of interest because other objectives had replaced it. I got in top shape and actually began making progress in my speed and power. I became expert at working around injuries and age limitations. I began living the maxim, "Don't worry about what you can't do, but concentrate on what you can do."

Along with my goals for the martial arts, I also made goals for writing, vacations, education, and my family. They weren't hastily made and quickly forgotten New Year's resolutions, but definite destinations to work toward. When I reached a short-term goal, I'd replace it with the middle-term goal, which I'd replace with a long-term goal. Then I would create a new long-term one.

Every time I reached one, I always took a couple days off to feel good about my accomplishment, and then I'd set a new goal.

Today, I'm a firm advocate of having a young attitude. Many super achievers at the age of seventy and eighty say, "You are only as old as you think you are." It's important to accept that there will be limitations, but it's also important to know that there will be new strengths. Yes, there are some things I no longer do as well in the martial arts, but I don't dwell on them because I'm constantly discovering other things I can do better because of my age. While my senior students may have some techniques that are stronger and faster than mine (a fact that I'm proud of as a teacher), my years of experience have given me a few tricks up my sleeve. (The junkyard dog didn't get to be an old dog because he's dumb.)

I like to think that I'm smarter at fifty-five than I was at twenty-five. I no longer practice fancy techniques in order to draw those "oohs" and "aahs." Now, my training is basic and practical, always with the acronym KISS, Keep It Simple Stupid, dangling in front of my eyes. Why kick to the head when I can drop an assailant with a powerful kick to the thigh?

As someone once wrote, "Growing old isn't for sissies." This is true, but with a little thought and a lot of work, it can be the best of times.

LET THE CHILDREN CHOOSE

Carrie is my oldest, born two months premature and weighing in at four pounds; she had a hard fight her first month just to stay alive. Dan arrived less than two years later, a big kid, anxious to get dirty and toss around a ball. Three years later, Amy joined us, a wonderful surprise because, though I wanted a girl, the doctors said it was going to be a boy.

From the day each child was born, I had little doubt they would someday be black belts. The martial arts have been a major part of my life since 1965, and I wanted my children to experience the same thing. When they were toddlers, I let them watch me train in the basement, and I would take them to my karate school to watch my classes. My hope was that they would be enthralled at what they were seeing and that they would try to emulate the movements. The reality was that they were not terribly interested. They would watch for a while, but then become bored and want to do something else.

When Dan was about eight years old, I made him join my class. He learned as well as the average child, but I could tell his heart wasn't in it. He talked incessantly about football and basketball, but never about karate. After just six weeks he called from his mother's house and left a message on my answering machine. "Hi dad, this is Dan. I don't want to do karate anymore. It's boring. Bye." My heart was broken. My dream of my only son following in my footsteps, shattered. Making it even worse was that he thought what I had devoted over half my life to was boring.

Three years later, Amy at five-and-a-half, told me she wanted to begin training. I couldn't believe it. I asked if she was sure, and she nodded yes, with a serious expression that looked out of place on her normally smiling face. She had been going to the karate school with me for two years, but she had always gone to the nursery room during my class. Occasionally, she would ask if she could stay in the training area where she would sit next to the wall, color pictures and give only a passing glance at the goings on. I couldn't detect even a spark of interest.

Before she could change her mind, I put Amy into a kids' class. I need not have worried, though, because she liked the training, both in the class and during the one-on-one with me at home. She thought the idea of earning different colored belts was fun, and she talked about someday earning her black belt. The more enthusiasm she had, the more thrilled I became.

Five months from the day she began, Amy earned her first belt, and six months after that she earned her second. She entered two tournaments when she was six years old, winning first place in both. Her techniques were fast and surprisingly powerful for a six year old.

Carrie was now twelve and Dan eleven. Just as I was about to give up hope that they would ever train, I came up with an idea. I talked to their mother about putting them in my class for just three months, the average time it takes older kids and adults to earn the first belt. If after that they wanted to quit, that would be okay, but the deal was they had to stay the entire three months. Their mother agreed.

The kids were not happy when I told them of the plan, but they agreed to try. My hope was now that they were older they would like karate as much as Amy, and my dream of all three kids being involved would be a reality. Dan turned out to be a good student, learning at an even pace. He practiced hard in class and accepted the extra training I gave him at home without complaint. But he never committed himself as to whether he would continue training after the three months.

Training Carrie was a disaster. She had never been interested in anything physical, choosing to spend her energy on academics and a myriad of school committees. While she always came to class, it was obvious she didn't want to be there. She acted silly and disruptive, and she pretended not to understand the material. I fought with her in school and we fought about it at home until my patience was exhausted. It was clear that she wasn't learning anything and all my scolding and threatening wasn't having an effect on her. I decided it was better for both of us that she was allowed to quit. I was divorced from her mother so our time together was limited; I didn't want karate to ruin our relationship by placing a wedge between us.

I sat Carrie down and told her that if she didn't want to continue, she didn't have to. I even put on a little sad face hoping it would make her feel guilty, but I barely had the words out of my mouth before she gave me a hug, said she loved me, and that she definitely wanted out of karate.

Our relationship improved immediately.

At the end of the three months, silent Dan passed his belt test and then announced that he wanted to continue training. I was happy he made that decision, but I was beginning to feel differently about the entire issue of karate and my children. Karate had taken me around the world, brought a certain amount of recognition, friendships, health, discipline, and has helped me learn about myself. It was only natural that I wanted my children to experience the same thing. When I really thought about it, however, and was completely honest, I realized that while I wanted it for them, I also wanted them to be little carbon copies of me to satisfy my ego, and as a way for me to stay young and immortal by living vicariously through them.

Like most parents, I tried to expose my children to as many diverse experiences as possible, but trying to force Carrie to do something that was against her nature was wrong. When it finally dawned on me what I had been doing to all the kids, I stopped, and I never again forced any of them to do something just because their old man did it. If they wanted to do the same things I did as they grew up, fine, but if they didn't, that was fine, too; it was more important to me that they grow into the adults they wanted to be. I would always be there for guidance, to offer suggestions and options so they could see the total picture, but the final choice would be theirs.

The years have passed and the kids grew. Amy earned her black belt when she was eighteen, and is now busy in college where she is majoring in primary education. She still practices the martial arts as a way to stay in shape. It's not paramount in her life, but rather one of many aspects of it. It's up to her how long she continues to do it.

Dan is in his twenties now. He quit karate training after three years, which disappointed me because he was beginning to show signs of being an excellent student. When he made the decision to quit and move on to basketball, which was always his first love, I supported him and let him go. He is a pastor now at a local church, married, and continuing his education in theology.

Carrie never returned to class. She is 26 at this writing and working on her masters degree in New York. For years now, she has worked with kids who have special education needs, and she plans to make her place in the world of social work.

Kelly, my twelve-year-old stepdaughter, is tall, athletic and strong. Although she is surrounded by the martial arts in our daily lives, she has shown no real interest in it at this time. Will she? I don't know. If she does, I'll teach her. But if she never shows interest, that's okay. It's her choice.

A LITTLE RED TROPHY

Looking back on it now, I shouldn't have been sparring that student. I had been working long hours at my police job, some nights not getting off duty until 2a.m. At 9a.m., I would drag myself out of bed to get to my school where I taught three classes and trained right along with the students. In early afternoon, I would dash home, clean up and head to the precinct for another extra-long shift. On the day of the accident, I was bone tired from two weeks of this schedule.

I had only been sparring a few minutes when I launched a fast, turning back kick. Half way into the spin, my fatigued support leg collapsed, and down I went. I learned later that my knee joint had dislocated, sending my kneecap on a tissue-tearing journey part way to the backside of my leg, chipping off part of the cap on the way. The pain was excruciating, and then some.

A couple of hours later, my leg was in a splint and my life was going to change in a big way. Unable to go to work and unable to train, I sat in an easy chair – all day long. Some nights, I even slept in it because the pain was too great to make the effort to hobble on my crutches into the bedroom.

Three months went by and my knee hadn't improved. I went to four doctors and they all told me it was a bad sprain and that

127

only time would heal it. One even said that because I was so physical and aware of my body, I was feeling more pain than a sprain should cause. In other words, the pain was in my head. But a fifth doctor found the problem. "It's hurting so much because your kneecap is broken," he said, shaking his head in disbelief that the other doctors hadn't found the problem. He rushed me into surgery, after which I stumbled around for three more months wearing a cast that stretched from my ankle to my hip. I spent a lot of time in my chair again, not working and not training.

After the cast came off and I had been sweating through physical therapy for a few weeks, the doctor broke the news. He said the damage to the muscles, tendons, tissue and joint had been so traumatic that I would never again walk without a cane and I would probably have to retire from the police department. For sure, he said, I would never again train in the martial arts.

I was more than emotionally shattered. At only twenty-eight, I was just informed that my police career was over and my beloved training, which had captivated me for nine years, was over, too. I couldn't begin to think what I would do with my life. The physical therapy was acutely painful and progress was slow, if at all. The world was getting darker each day as I sank deeper and deeper into depression.

One day as I was driving home from a physical therapy session, one in which my progress had regressed, sinking me even further into my self-pity, when that proverbial bolt from the sky zapped me. Where it came from and why it struck just then, I haven't a clue, but in the blink of an eye, I suddenly saw myself objectively, and it disgusted me. "Just stop it!" I said aloud in my car. "This stops now!" Then louder and with total commitment, "I'm going back to work and I'm going to train again. I'm going to prove that doctor wrong."

I never went back to physical therapy. I continued doing one of the exercises at home and added two martial arts exercises for the legs, allowing for a day's rest between the workouts, something the therapists hadn't given me. Within two weeks, I began to see and feel progress for the first time since I had been injured.

Along with the physical improvement came a much-improved mental outlook. Every small gain strengthened my conviction that I would once again do those things that I loved. The goal was a tough one that would be a long and painful journey, but I was driven to do whatever it took to make it happen.

Six months later I was back doing police work. It was a desk job, but I had improved enough for them to let me come back, minus the cane. A year later, I was in good enough shape to once again work street patrol.

I didn't return to the martial arts for a couple of years because while creating exercises for my leg, I got interested in bodybuilding. I eventually improved to where I could do heavy leg extensions and barbell squats with three hundred and fifty pounds. Squatting that poundage is insignificant for a guy my size, but considering that I was told two years earlier that I would probably always have to use a cane, I felt pretty darn good about it. I even got in good enough shape to enter the Mr. Oregon contest, though I wasn't much of a threat to those who won.

I returned to training through the Filipino martial art of arnis. I was concerned at first because with weight training, I controlled the exercise motion, which minimized the risk to my knee. But with martial arts training, there was a greater risk because there were sudden turns, spins, squats and jumps. The instructor, who was also a friend, knew about my knee and thought I could do it. He was right. Although some of the stances hurt and some nights my knee swelled, I ate the pain and kept at it.

For the next two years, I studied arnis, tai chi, kung fu and karate. The pain eventually diminished and my legs grew stronger than ever. One day, a tournament announcement caught my attention. Could I do it? Would my leg give out as it still did once or twice a week? Would I embarrass myself in front of the crowd? Would I... "Just stop it," I said aloud. I could keep asking these stall-tactic questions or I could continue to think positive and start training for the competition. I chose the latter.

Two months later I was at the tournament, competing in forms competition against ten other black belts. When it was all over, I was on the winner's platform, standing in the fourth place position, holding a little red and ornate, eight-inch-high trophy. As small and insignificant as the little trophy looked to others, it meant more to me than the fifty other trophies and the belt promotions that would follow over the next few years.

Today, that little trophy has a special place in my den, so that whenever life gets tough, which is does with absolute certainty, I look at it and remember what the warrior spirit can do.

THE TEST

My jujitsu instructor and friend, Professor Tim Delgman, called me one day from where he lives in San Francisco and said that he wanted me to prepare to test for my second-degree black belt in jujitsu. He said it would be a tough one that would test my knowledge of technique and challenge my physical condition.

He wanted to see fifty advanced techniques, each containing a combination of two to four grappling moves interspersed with karate kicks and punches. There would also be defense against gun, knife and club attacks, as well defense against punches, chokes, grabs and multiple opponents. He wanted most of the techniques executed while standing, though there would be a few I would demonstrate while on my back.

I wasn't worried about the combination techniques, but I was concerned about having to spar against multiple opponents — first one, then two, then three and then all four at the same time. The attackers could use anything: karate, boxing and jujitsu, but I had to use mostly jujitsu in my defense, with the occasional kick or punch. It was going to be tough, requiring good aerobic conditioning and fast reflexes.

Six weeks prior to the test, I began intensifying my practice sessions, working hard with opponents as well as simulating movements in the air by myself. My primary objective was to improve my endurance, an area that had always been a weakness.

I began training using three, two-minute rounds. Whether pantomiming in the air or training with a real opponent, I worked on a variety of attacks and defenses, executing the moves as fast and intensely as I could. I'd go nonstop for two minutes, rest a minute, and then go another two minutes. The second week I increased to five, two-minute rounds, the third week to seven rounds and the fourth week, to ten rounds. The last two weeks, I increased all of the rounds to three minutes, though the test required only four, two-minute rounds. My wind improved dramatically, and I felt confident I could handle anything that was asked of me.

Professor Delgman flew in from California the day of the test. The professor is a big, thickly built man, who holds eight black belts in jujitsu and a black belt in karate. His grappling skills are extraordinary and, if an attacker should try to make him a victim, the hapless fellow would experience more pain than any human should.

We spent the afternoon talking about jujitsu and what he expected from me during the test, which would begin at 7:00p.m.. I was apprehensive about the test and also nervous about all my students and friends coming to watch. By 6:00p.m. my stomach was doing flip-flops.

The June day was unseasonably hot, somewhere in the high nineties, so within minutes of putting on my heavy canvas uniform and doing a few warm-up exercises, I was dripping with sweat. My students set up three large fans, but they had no effect against the still-blazing sun that poured through the seven-foot-high wall of windows.

The test began with a demonstration of ten single techniques. I went through each movement slowly to show what the move was

131

and then a second time at full speed. I drew deeply into myself to put my warrior spirit into each hold, kick and punch. After ten minutes, I was pouring sweat but my strength and endurance had never been better. In fact, I seemed to be growing stronger as the test progressed.

Thirty minutes later, I was demonstrating combinations containing three techniques, and though my endurance still felt good, my profuse sweating was starting to bother me. Although, I wasn't used to wearing a heavy canvas uniform jacket, since we always wore T-shirts in my school, it still seemed that I was sweating more than I should. Maybe, I thought, I'm coming down with something.

It happened about five minutes later when I was in the middle of executing a triple. The attack was a hard face punch. I blocked it, grabbed my opponent's wrist, slammed a roundhouse kick into his chest, and foot-swept him to the ground. To control him, I hyperextended his elbow across my knee and pressed my thumb into a sensitive nerve under his jawbone. Just as I looked up to see if the professor was satisfied or wanted me to repeat the move, a sudden wave of weakness washed over me from head to toes. The sensation was similar to that horrible feeling just before vomiting: nausea, goose bumps, sweating, and weakness. I have no idea where it came from, but it struck harder and faster than any of the blows coming at me.

The professor wanted to see the combination again and at combat speed, after which the horrible feeling intensified. I didn't think it was possible to sweat more, but it poured, and a moment later I was gasping for air. If this had happened during a class, I would have asked a senior student to take over so I could sit down or go home. But this wasn't a class. It was an event in which a lot of people had come to watch and for which my instructor had flown in from out of town. I had to go on.

The next section was ground defenses, in which I had to lay on my back and defend against several types of attacks: punches, chokes and various grappling holds. There was nothing difficult about the techniques, except that they drained my already dissipating energy and strength. Somehow, I survived the section, but as I lay there for a moment afterwards, I began having serious doubts as to how much longer I could go on. I struggled to get up on shaking legs.

The test wore on: club attacks, knife attacks, chokes, gun defense and a large section of miscellaneous attacks. I was able to execute my techniques with sufficient power and speed, but in between, as the next attack was being called out, I was dying. The room spun, my knees buckled a couple of times, and my breath came out in slobbering gasps. I asked for, and received begrudgingly, a two-minute break, which I spent on my knees in front of the fans. I opened my jacket to allow the wind to cool the overheated "oven" underneath, but it didn't help, and getting back up was a giant effort.

Next: sparring, the king of the energy drainers.

It was as if I had two people inside of me debating. One was shouting a warning that I would certainly die if I continued, while the other one encouraged me to stay in there. I hated that second guy, the annoyingly positive one, but I followed his advice.

I faced my opponent and bowed slowly, wondering for a moment if I was going to be able to straighten back up. My body felt as if it weighed five hundred pounds, a quarter ton of sweat spouting, quivering Jello. He attacked with a driving punch; I sidestepped, whipped my forearm across his throat and swept him onto his back. He leapt to his feet and launched a kick, which I grabbed and twisted, spiraling him to the floor. The two minutes seemed like two days until Professor Delgman finally called halt.

I reached out and grabbed the wall as the room tilted and my head swam in nausea. Focusing on the big fans, as if they were a cool, refreshing oasis in a blistering desert, I staggered across the room and bent before them, my hands on my shaking knees. "It...will be over in just a few... more minutes," the positive voice whispered. "A few...more minutes."

133

"Two attackers!" the Professor called out, and the two charged without hesitation. Again, I fought back, my strength coming from some mysterious place. "Stop!" the professor called after two long minutes. I survived again, though I could barely remember sparring. I had stopped sweating, too, which is never a good sign.

Three opponents stepped forward. I could barely lift my arms into a fighting stance as I struggled to focus on their images that seemed to float in and out of a thick mist. Someone grabbed me from behind, but I didn't have the strength to shake him off; all I wanted to do was fall down. I kicked feebly at a blurry image to my front. I sensed someone coming at me from my side and I threw the man holding me into him. Whatever I did that worked was not the result of my physical strength, but rather the mechanics of the ancient techniques that had been ingrained in me.

"Four attackers!" the Professor called out, without allowing for the two-minute break. I fought them as if my life depended on it, which in my delirious mind, it did. My punches and kicks were thrown uncontrolled, but it didn't matter because most were landing too weakly to hurt anyone, anyway. I threw opponents into each other so that they would trip and fall together. The fewer I had to contend with, the less energy I had to expend. At one point, my back was pressed against the wall, and though I fought with all my remaining strength, my attackers were getting the best of me.

Then, what little physical and mental strength I had, rushed out me like air from a punctured balloon. I couldn't breath and I could no longer move. All four attackers were on me, psyched that their punches and kicks were landing uncontrolled, and hard. One of them had hold of my head and was pulling me down. My mind commanded my muscles to move, but they were deaf. I tried, I willed, but nothing happened.

A thought raced through my mind that I could have a heart attack. I no longer cared what anyone thought; I just wanted this to be over.

Just as I wheezed out, "That's all, no more," the Professor called for it to end. Later, he said he didn't hear me say anything, so maybe I only uttered the words in my mind. He told me to take a break while he looked at his notes. Without acknowledging the applause from my friends and students, I staggered to my office, shut the door and spiraled to the floor in a heap of groaning flesh. I tried to get up, but a giant, invisible weight pressed me into the floor, deeper and deeper.

I don't know how long I lay there or how long the voice had been calling me from the other side of the door. When it finally penetrated the thick delirium in my brain, I recognized it as one of my students; he was telling me that the Professor was ready.

I must have gotten up because my next memory is of walking into the training room and over to my instructor. He called me to attention, made a few comments that didn't register in my brain, and then announced that I had passed the test and was promoted to the rank of Nidan, second-degree black belt in jujitsu.

I'm guessing I had contracted a touch of the flu that day, as I had flu-like symptoms for several hours after. It definitely wasn't a result of poor conditioning because I was in good shape and confident I could meet the rigors of the test. What I know for sure is that it was my warrior spirit that kept me going as long as I did.

But what happened at the end of the test? I have always believed and taught that people could continue to fight if they just reached inside themselves and pulled out that part of the warrior spirit called "will." I did manage to pull it out for a while, but in the end, I no longer had it. Hard as I tried, I couldn't find it.

Let's look at some "what ifs." What if I had been stabbed on the street and the wound weakened me to the same extent I was weakened at the end of the test? What if my attacker then moved in to finish the job? Would I be able to bring out more warrior spirit to defend my life? What if the stabber were to take advantage of my condition and hurt someone in my family? Could I then bring on more fight?

My immediate answer is yes, but I'm answering these questions on a day when I feel strong, well rested, and have lots of energy.

What if during the last thirty seconds of my jujitsu test, the Professor had told me to continue fighting because this time the attackers were really going to try to kill me or hurt someone in my family? Could I have done it?

Remembering how completely debilitated I was...

So, is there a point where a person no longer has the will to continue, no matter what the threat? If there is, does that mean that the warrior spirit can die?

I'm not sure.

CONCLUSION

I'm writing this Conclusion in a spiral notebook while sprawled in the shade of a grove of 75-foot-high palm trees on a secluded beach in Kona, Hawaii. Life doesn't get much better than this: clear blue skies, lazy ocean swells, the melodic sounds of brilliantly plumed exotic birds, and a sensuous breeze on which rides the perfume of a dozen varieties of tropical flowers.

It seems rather incongruous to be vacationing in paradise and writing my final thoughts about all the explosive violence, unbridled rage, stomach churning fear, acts of courage and acts of stupidity that are chronicled in the stories that precede these final words.

I was about to write that from the vantage point of this spectacular place these memories don't seem real. But that thought lasted only a moment, because all I have to do is close my eyes and Drill Sergeant Collier, Sampson, Weak Jaw, Karen, the headless psychiatrist and the escaped prisoner, emerge out of the dark, one after the other, all looking just as they did when I last saw them. Upon opening my eyes, I see the scars of many battles on my hands, a finger that was never set straight after it was broken, a seven-inch surgery scar on a knee, and a shin dotted with marks where shotgun pellets entered and exited. When I attempt to speak at a higher pitch than normal, only a breathy squeak comes out, the result of a vocal cord damaged from an opponent's spinning hook kick. All of this tangible evidence (for purposes of continuity, the stories behind some of the injuries weren't told here), remind me that the memories of my adventures of the warrior spirit are most definitely real.

Actually, mine pale when compared with what occurred in 1779, only a short distance from my seemingly peaceful place here in the shade, when English explorer Captain James Cook and his ships the *Resolution* and the *Discovery* engaged in a fierce battle with Hawaiians. The sailors fought with muskets, the Hawaiians with spears and stones, as the sea turned red with the blood of those injured and killed on both sides. The last act of Captain Cook was to try to swim to safety, but before he was able, a dozen Hawaiians surrounded him and bludgeoned him to death.

Now, over 200 years later, my wife and I are enjoying a pampered week-long vacation in a six-story, ultra-modern hotel built on a lava flow just a few yards from where waves lap at the shore, waves that once carried blood from Captain Cook's battle.

The hotel was not built by spear-toting warriors, but rather by modern day, latte drinking, stressed out corporate executives, who used their warrior spirits and laptop computers to do battle with bankers, architects and contractors. Now that the hotel is built, its owners and managers continue to call upon their warrior spirits to aggressively attract tenants, compete for the best work crews, and battle with loaning institutions for capital to make upgrades.

For sure, no matter where you are and no matter what you do, it is with you. Whether you are on the board of directors of a hotel here in sun-drenched paradise, a cop pulling the midnight shift in a high-crime area of Detroit, a high school student on a track team in Los Angeles, a housewife in Des Moines, a soldier in some remote, troubled country, or a beginning or advanced martial artist anywhere, your warrior spirit is with you, to help or to hinder, depending on your mind set.

As I noted in the Introduction, my purpose in sharing these personal stories is so that you might find a little of yourself in them. Who is the "Sampson" in your life? What have you learned about yourself when you have enjoyed a moment in the sun or when you have had to eat a piece of humble pie?

It's important to think about and analyze your experiences so that you develop an understanding of your warrior spirit, and by understanding it, you learn to control it, tame it if necessary, and then use it for good. But be warned: Even after you understand it, or think you do, you must never let down your guard; you must remain ever vigilant.

For after all, your warrior spirit is a crouching tiger.

Warriorhood is a path, not a destination.

About the Author

Loren W. Christensen has lived the life of a warrior.

He began his martial arts career in 1965 and continues to teach and write about street oriented self defense. He has written 14 books on the fighting arts, made two videos on police defensive tactics, written dozens of magazine articles on realistic fighting, and consults with various organizations on matters of security and self defense.

In 1967, Loren joined the army and served as a military policeman in the United States and in Saigon, Vietnam. In 1972, he joined the Portland (Oregon) Police Bureau where he worked as a street officer, bodyguard, defensive tactics instructor, and an expert on street gangs, specializing in white supremacists.

Loren's varied experiences have brought him face to face with the crouching tiger, the warrior spirit that resides in each one of us.

Loren can be contacted through his web site at www.lwcbooks.com.